Winning Beyond Boundaries

NARROWCAST - 4th EDITION

Blume Ventures

wyzr

Published by Wyzr Content Pvt. Ltd.

ISBN (Paperback): 978-81-964817-2-8
ISBN (Hardback): 978-81-964817-8-0
ISBN (eBook): 978-81-964817-3-5

Typeset in Adobe InDesign by Amlan Chakravarty

Cover by Ann Mathew

Printed and bound by Gopsons Papers Pvt. Ltd., Noida
First printing edition 2025

Contents

Section 3 - Sportspersons

Preface

The moment hung suspended in time.

As Neeraj Chopra's javelin pierced through the Tokyo sky in 2021 (remember, Tokyo 2020 eventually happened in 2021 due to the pandemic), it wasn't just breaking Olympic records; it was shattering boundaries that had constrained Indian aspirations for generations.

That golden throw showcased that India was ready to not just compete on the world stage but win in it.

As investors, we are seeing this sentiment cut across the startup ecosystem. Indian founders are no longer content with dominating domestic markets. They're aiming for the stars and landing among them. This year's theme, 'Winning Beyond Boundaries,' examines how the newfound Indian confidence and aspirations are manifesting on the global stage.

From Girish Mathrubootham ringing the NASDAQ bell for Freshworks to GreyOrange's robots orchestrating global warehouses to Ultrahuman's rings tracking consumer health across 150 countries, Indian innovation is breaking barriers with unprecedented confidence.

Mind you, this transformation runs deeper.

It marks India's evolution from the world's back office to its innovation frontier.

Through the voices of Harsh Mariwala, who showed what it takes to build global consumer brands; Amitabh Kant, who elevated India into a must-visit tourism destination; and Mahesh Bhupathi, who pioneered Indian excellence in Grand Slams, these stories share one message: the world ain't seen nothing yet.

Join us as we explore how Anand Deshpande built Persistent into a billion-dollar product engineering powerhouse, how Aditya Ghosh transformed Indian aviation at IndiGo (and doing it again at Akasa Air), how Mukund Rajan shaped the Tata global brand, and how Alok Sama drove Softbank's strategic vision.

As you turn these pages, you'll discover that these aren't just individual success stories but blueprints for generations to follow and win beyond boundaries.

Welcome to a future where Indian innovation and leadership reshape the world.

Happy Reading!

Chapter 1
Introduction

Winning Beyond Boundaries - A Conversation with Blume Ventures' Karthik Reddy

In an insightful conversation, Karthik Reddy, Managing Partner and Co-founder of Blume Ventures, discusses the transformative journey of Indian startups from local players to global contenders.

He shares his perspectives on the evolving confidence of Indian entrepreneurs, the significance of Blume's "Winning Beyond Boundaries" philosophy, and how companies are making their mark on the international stage.

The discussion reveals how India's business ecosystem has matured from its IT services-led export heritage to building world-class products and brands that compete against the best brands in the world and win.

What does 'Winning Beyond Boundaries' mean to you?

Every year, we consider what defines the success of Blume companies and Indian startups. Recently, there has been a surge of confidence in our startups and portfolio companies building brands and businesses overseas.

Historically, India has exported commodities, manufacturing, and built an IT services behemoth by exporting talent. For the first time, India is poised to export new-age products, from consumer internet apps and games to tangible products. This insight inspired everything we've done in 2024, starting with the Blume Day 2024 theme.

This translated into two slogans. Our T-shirt proclaimed, 'You ain't seen nothing yet,' suggesting that the world has yet to witness India's full potential on the global stage, not just in the Olympics but also in the business world. The second aspect focused on showcasing our best examples, which led to the tagline 'Winning Beyond Boundaries.' This tagline highlights the best Indian entrepreneurship, culture, and role models who have succeeded overseas and created pathways for others.

What changes have you seen in the Indian startup ecosystem in the last few years?

The talent has become bolder. While this might have seemed a natural progression after 20 years of IT services, we had to overcome our complexes. Indians have an affinity for well-designed global brands and software products from overseas. We needed outsiders to validate our products' quality before Indians took pride in this journey and realized their own potential.

These changes are now evident. We're seeing the first product software unicorns, consumer deep-tech unicorns, and consumer unicorns. This transformation took a 10-year cycle. From 2010 to 2020, investing in such talent, though sporadic, created a virtuous cycle where talent now has the courage to compete globally.

The second change is our natural integration into the global market. Whether through Amazon, Shiprocket, or our Express logistics companies, the ability to reach global markets has transformed. App stores and the internet have simplified distribution compared to 15 years ago, moving away from mainframes and labor-intensive export processes.

Third, brand India is growing stronger. When culture moves at unprecedented speed and scale, it creates opportunities. This pattern built the United States and Japan. Every brand represents something; we represent vibrancy and technology, which translates into our products. From Sabyasachi in Paris to Forest Essentials in London, Indian brands are reaching every corner of the world.

Capital must believe in this potential, role models must emerge, and we must leverage our talent for world-class manufacturing. We've overcome the perception that China had won the race. After viewing markets like Southeast Asia or China as distant competitors for 15-20 years, our founders now recognize they can build and manufacture products of equal quality in India.

Which Blume portfolio companies are riding the global wave?

While we initially expected product software companies to go global, our first batch struggled due to limited capital for U.S. expansion. Over the last decade, companies like Freshworks, Chargebee, and Zenoti have become unicorns, inspiring a new generation.

For Blume, early success came through deep tech winners like GreyOrange and Carbon Clean. College graduates built solutions for Western hemisphere challenges in warehouse automation and carbon capture. Enterprise software and SaaS are now established sectors, with initiatives like SaaSBoomi becoming prominent.

What's remarkable is our ability to build cutting-edge manufacturing companies like Ethereal Machines that sell overseas and take our strengths in healthcare to global customers through companies like Healthify and Ultrahuman. Ultrahuman now generates only 15 percent of its revenue from India and has sold rings in 150 countries, a scale that seemed impossible three or four years ago.

Lastly, consumer brands are gaining momentum. We're seeing the first D2C brands, born just 5-10 years ago, selling globally.

Section 1
Founders

Chapter 2
From Troll to Triumph

How Freshworks conquered global SaaS from India

"Freshworks is the company that wasn't supposed to win," declared the company's blog after its historic NASDAQ listing on September 22, 2021.

After all, it was the 605th helpdesk software in the world when it launched on October 13, 2010.

Conventional wisdom suggested it was already too late. The market was saturated and dominated by established players. A SaaS company from India had no business competing globally.

This skepticism wasn't just whispered—it was public and brutal.

In a particularly telling exchange from December 2012, Ben Kepes, a prominent cloud analyst and Zendesk blogger, publicly labeled Freshdesk (as Freshworks was called then) a "troll" on X (then Twitter).

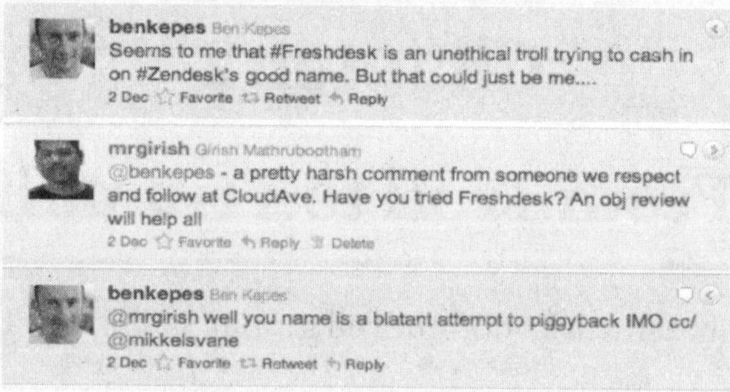

benkepes Ben Kepes
Seems to me that #Freshdesk is an unethical troll trying to cash in on #Zendesk's good name. But that could just be me....
2 Dec Favorite Retweet Reply

mrgirish Girish Mathrubootham
@benkepes - a pretty harsh comment from someone we respect and follow at CloudAve. Have you tried Freshdesk? An obj review will help all
2 Dec Favorite Reply Delete

benkepes Ben Kepes
@mrgirish well you name is a blatant attempt to piggyback IMO cc/ @mikkelsvane
2 Dec Favorite Retweet Reply

Things took an even uglier turn when Ben Kepes' follower Christian Marth (@cloudgroupsyd) said the below.

cloudgroupsyd Christian Marth
@benkepes bunch of Indian cowboys #freshdesk
2 Dec

mrgirish Girish Mathrubootham
@cloudgroupsyd Making an unsolicited attack on our nationality reflects badly on u, not us. We're Indian and we're proud of that.
2 Dec Favorite Reply Delete

cloudgroupsyd Christian Marth
@mrgirish not attacking your nationality only your lack of innovation for product development, if you were offended in any way sorry
2 Dec

mrgirish Girish Mathrubootham
@cloudgroupsyd Have you tried Freshdesk? It's 6 months old now. I'm sure both of us will be around to see how this plays out.
2 Dec Favorite Reply Delete

To add the cherry on top, Mikkel Svane, co-founder and the then-CEO of Zendesk, entered the chat.

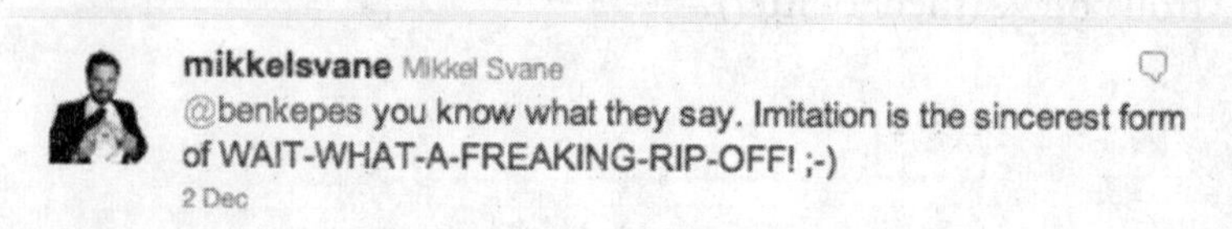

mikkelsvane Mikkel Svane
@benkepes you know what they say. Imitation is the sincerest form of WAIT-WHAT-A-FREAKING-RIP-OFF! ;-)
2 Dec

If this barrage of criticism wasn't enough, a Forbes contributor delivered what seemed like the final blow in 2014:

"Zendesk. Autotask. Freshdesk. These are three great little companies that make three excellent help desk/customer service management applications. But they, like others in this niche, could be in trouble," said a Forbes article titled 'Microsoft Just Put These 3 Companies Out Of Business'.

This article was written when Microsoft acquired the cloud-based customer engagement platform Parature for USD100 million.

A decade of relentless execution later, the "troll" has transformed into a global SaaS powerhouse. With USD686 million in trailing twelve-month revenue (as of November 2024), nearly 5,000 employees worldwide, and over 68,000 customers, Freshworks is well on its way to reaching USD 1 billion in revenue.

What happened in the last decade and a half is a masterclass in building a global technology company from India. Freshworks not only silenced its critics but also created a new playbook for Indian founders building for the world from India, achieving what most believed could not be done.

Today, Freshworks is, without a doubt, the true benchmark for the Indian SaaS ecosystem. Tiruchirapalli-born Girish Mathrubootham, the enigmatic founder and executive chairman of Freshworks, is India SaaS' OG founder.

Here are G's (as Girish is fondly called) top-earned secrets about what made him and Freshworks click.

Lesson 1 - Capital allocation is an art: Know where every dollar drives growth and where frugality builds strength.

Freshworks' first backer, Shekhar Kirani, partner at the Indian arm of the global venture capital firm Accel, made an astute observation when he first met Girish and the early team in their 700-square-foot office space in Chennai. Their furniture was a mix and match of different types of tables and chairs; the design was a bit all over the place, but everyone had Macs.

"It signaled to me that the guys knew where to spend money," he said in an earlier interview.

Girish's mantra (which he learned from his mentor Kumar Vembu of Zoho) is rather simple yet profound—just because there's money to spend doesn't mean you have to.

Girish has followed it across his many endeavors.

Take, for example, FC Madras, the football academy he owns, whose vision is to find the 'next Messi from Madras.'

"Even at FC Madras, everything you see on the pitch is world-class. The hostels are functional—they're good but not lavish. So I think that's a mindset every founder should know," said Girish.

He drives home this point further with an analogy about capital allocation and fitness.

> *"When you have unhealthy eating habits, and you're not paying attention to what you're eating, you end up becoming unhealthy. The same happens with many VC-funded startups—you're loading up on*

money and spending without knowing what you're getting for it. You end up becoming an unhealthy business."

Girish emphasizes that capital allocation is the primary responsibility of a growth stage or, for that matter, a public company CEO.

"Every quarter and every year, you have to review how capital is being used. Where are you deploying it, and what returns are you getting? Which areas deserve more investment to accelerate growth, and which ones should you exit?"

Lesson 2 - Learn to spot pockets of blue ocean inside a red ocean

Remember, Freshdesk was the 605th helpdesk in the world? It was a red ocean with numerous competitors. Freshworks (then Freshdesk) had to create its own 'pockets' of blue ocean in the 'red ocean'.

At the heart of it was the departure from the conventional enterprise software playbook.

To explain Freshworks' innovative Go-To-Market (GTM) motion, Girish first breaks down the conventional enterprise GTM playbook, "The typical enterprise software business model is straightforward: you start in one country—usually the US—building software for large companies. You hire a substantial sales team, and they go out to meet customers and close deals. You need to make small talk about baseball and weather, and it's very hard to do that (for non-Americans)," said Girish.

Navigating cultural nuances and building personal relationships are challenging and resource-intensive for a young Indian startup.

Instead, Freshworks pioneered an "inbound acquisition model"—what the industry would later term Product-led Growth (PLG).

"But what if the customer is not talking to you but is experiencing the product first?" said Girish.

This approach flipped the script on customer acquisition. Rather than relying on a field sales team to pitch the product, meet multiple stakeholders in a company, negotiate the annual contract price, and sign the contract, Freshworks let the product speak for itself.

By doing so, Freshworks bypassed the cultural barriers and high costs associated with traditional face-to-face sales. It also enabled them to go global from day one. "When we had seven customers, they came from four different continents," Girish recounted.

This global approach was revolutionary for an Indian startup at the time, opening up a vast market opportunity that wasn't constrained by geographical boundaries.

Freshworks doubled down on its product and user experience to make it as easy to use as someone sitting next to the customer and explaining the features.

> *"We used an affordable price, intuitive, easy-to-use, and full-featured product as a combination to get the 'wow' from the customer before they even speak to somebody," said Girish.*

This product-led approach allowed Freshworks to establish product-market fit quickly, a fact that didn't go unnoticed by investors. Girish remembered what Shekhar had told him early into the Freshworks days.

"Shekhar told me—look, Girish, you have USD2,000 in revenue from 70 different SMB customers across the globe. That proves product-market fit. The only risk here is execution, and I'm comfortable with that."

This was Freshworks' blue ocean strategy in action—instead of competing head-on with established players in their traditional enterprise sales motion, they created a new market space through product-led growth. By focusing on SMB customers globally and letting the product sell itself, Freshworks turned what seemed like a disadvantage—being an Indian startup without a US sales presence—into their greatest strength.

Lesson 3 - The best time to expand your product portfolio is when you don't need to.

While most startups launch new products when the growth of their core product stagnates, Freshworks took a bolder approach. "We went multi-product when things were pretty early and going good," Girish explained. He added, "When times are tough, you'll be asked to cut costs. There won't be any bandwidth or resources left to actually start building."

Freshworks' multi-product strategy was rooted in a key insight about SMB behavior: these customers prefer sticking to one trusted vendor for all their software needs to avoid the complexity of managing multiple tools. This created tremendous headroom for growth.

> *"You are already my customer. We are the system of records platform for you. So, why should I give the opportunity for somebody else to build a small standalone tool," said Girish.*

Freshworks' multi-product strategy was both expansive and targeted. They started with Freshdesk for customer support and then expanded to Freshservice for employee IT support. Girish explained, "Freshdesk started with ticketing, email support, and a self-service knowledge base. We took that foundation to Freshservice for internal IT help desk, and later built more features for what IT teams needed."

They soon launched Freshsales, their CRM product. It was driven by the observation that many Freshdesk customers were integrating with CRM systems.

Girish noted, "For many of our customers using Freshdesk, their top integrations were for CRMs. CRM and customer support should ideally work very closely together, so we launched Freshsales."

Freshworks' multi-product strategy created rapid growth that wouldn't have been possible with a single product in the SMB market. "Freshworks went from USD 1 million to 5 million to 15 to 34 to 56. So that journey would not have been possible with only one product," added Girish.

The low cost of experimentation in India was a key enabler of this multi-product strategy. Girish explained, "The cost of an experiment for a startup in India is much lower than in the

US or Europe. I'm not talking about blitzscaling and burning millions. For us, an experiment meant 5 or 6 developers working on a project for 9 to 12 months, which came to less than USD 300K-500K."

Lesson 4 - I don't care about your degree. I want to find out what your talent is.

In Freshworks' early years, Girish encountered a major challenge: the scarcity of specialized talent in India.

He recalled, "I was trying to hire my first marketing person in 2011. It was incredibly hard to find somebody from India who had done software marketing globally. But in the Valley, I could find specialists in nine different disciplines of SaaS marketing—inbound, customer advocacy, digital, and field marketing."

To overcome this constraint, Freshworks adopted an innovative hiring and talent development approach.

Inspired by Marcus Buckingham and Curt Coffman's book, 'First, Break All The Rules', Girish developed a hiring philosophy focused on innate talent rather than specific skills or experience. He explained, "You have to learn to differentiate between skills, knowledge, and talent. Skills are easily teachable and learnable. Knowledge—there is factual knowledge, and there is experiential knowledge. Factual knowledge, again, is easily teachable. Over time, some of the experiential knowledge can become best practices. However, talent is not teachable. It's something you're born with."

This approach led to a hiring strategy that looked beyond traditional qualifications.

Girish assessed candidates on unconventional criteria. "Are you an unorganized creative person, or are you a very organized regimental person? Are you very articulate and enjoy talking to people, or are you introverted and you would rather not speak? Do you have empathy? Can you think on your feet?"

He continued, "If I'm hiring for customer support, I need to find someone with empathy and patience. For pre-sales, I need someone who can teach me new things and think on their feet when I adjust the audience level. For sales, I'll talk to you about multiple topics, and you have to make the conversation interesting. You have to be shameless—I'll ask you to sing or dance. You have to do that."

"These are natural traits. I don't care whether you're a biotech engineer or a computer science engineer. If I know who you are at your core, I can put you in the right role and groom you for it."

This talent-first approach allowed Freshworks to build a diverse and capable team despite the lack of industry-specific experience. "The first 70 programmers we hired weren't familiar with Ruby on Rails (the language on which Freshdesk is built) before joining Freshdesk," he said in an earlier interview.

As Freshworks matured and became a public company, the approach to talent acquisition evolved. Girish explained, "When we went public, we had a revenue of USD 300 million. To grow from USD 300 million to USD 3 billion or USD 5 billion, the hiring playbook had to change."

At this stage, Freshworks prioritized experience and expertise for certain roles. Girish noted, "For SEC compliance, I cannot hire somebody in Bangalore and say, 'we'll learn by doing.' One mistake will kill you. For taxation, we need a global tax expert. There's a whole organization needed to support a public company."

This shift in strategy also came with increased access to experienced talent pools in the US and Europe. "Now, with Freshworks in the US and Europe, we have access to the talent pool. I would be better off hiring somebody who has seen that scale—who has taken companies from USD200 million to USD2 billion multiple times," said Girish.

This evolution in hiring strategy reflects Freshworks' journey as a company. Freshworks demonstrated how to balance foundational principles with the practicalities of scaling. Girish's dual philosophy—building from within while bringing in experienced leaders—remains a key driver of Freshworks' continued success.

Lesson 5 - Get to a position to ask for 3x, not 30% more.

Girish Mathrubootham's fundraising strategy, very early in Freshworks' journey, offers a masterclass in strategic capital raising: raise capital when you don't need it and negotiate from a position of strength.

Shortly after securing the first round of funding from Accel, numerous investors approached Girish. Despite having money in the bank, he engaged in these conversations. However, when their terms didn't align with his vision for Freshworks, he didn't hesitate to push back.

His response to an offer at a 30% markup is particularly telling. "I look at Freshworks as a Valley company. I know how Zendesk and Desk.com raised their rounds. I don't need money now, but when I do my next round, I need a 3x multiple, not a 30% markup."

With this bold stance, Girish laid out what would become Freshworks' fundraising philosophy: benchmark against global leaders, not local peers; exercise patience even when investors are eager; set clear expectations about valuation upfront; and, most importantly, demonstrate unwavering confidence in your company's growth trajectory. It was a philosophy that would attract capital and the right kind of investors who shared this vision.

This approach paid off when Lee Fixel, who was then with Tiger Global, despite acknowledging that Freshworks was "very early" for their typical investments, decided to bet on Girish's vision and potential.

Girish recalled what Lee Fixel told him—"Girish, the numbers don't make any sense. You are very early for us as a fund. But I am making a bet on you. You have seen scale."

Freshworks went on to raise nearly USD500 million across multiple rounds, culminating in a ~USD10 billion market capitalization during the NASDAQ IPO. Looking back, Girish's strategy of thinking global from day one, raising capital from a position of strength, and setting Valley-level expectations had paid off. The company that started by refusing a modest 30% markup had successfully commanded valuations at par with its global SaaS peers.

Life comes full circle.

Remember how this story began? Freshworks was called out as a "troll," written off by competitors, and "wasn't supposed to win."

But a decade and half of stellar execution has a magical way of changing narratives. Freshworks not only proved critics wrong but also rewrote the rules for building world-class software products from India.

Ben Kepes, the same analyst who had once called them a "troll", sent what he called a "smoke signal of peace" to Freshworks in August 2022.

Ben Kepes
@benkepes

Sending a smoke signal of peace to my friends at @FreshworksInc from the @AWS Public Sector Summit. All forgiven now, @mrgirish ??? ;)

To which India's SaaS thalaiva replied,

Girish Mathrubootham @mrgirish · Aug 31, 2022
Where is the question of forgiving when you handed us gold with Ripoffornot.org
We @FreshworksInc are eternally grateful to you. So pls accept my sincere thanks that I couldn't say 11 yrs ago.

5 39 227

Ben Kepes @benkepes · Aug 31, 2022
LoL, think of me as your (weirdly) secret BDM. That website will haunt me forever, you realise

21

We thought it'd be best if we let Girish's words complete this chapter for us. This is from their blog after their listing (quoted above).

"Whether we could differentiate ourselves in crowded markets, or compete with larger players, or build a global SaaS company from India, ***the doubts were always there****. And people were not shy about telling me! Yet, we kept our heads down and focused on executing, focused on our mission. We realized the profound meaning of what Steve Jobs once said,* ***'Stay hungry, stay foolish'****."*

Freshworks is a very special company. We were unconventional from the beginning – not for its own sake, but because we saw an opening in the market for a unique approach.

We weren't founded in Silicon Valley. We didn't target large enterprises. We didn't have access to a been-there-done-that talent pool. We designed our products for the people actually using them. ***We offered a 'fresh' approach, and we serviced massive, underserved markets.***

I'm very proud that ***Freshworks is a pioneer of Indian entrepreneurship*** *and of our ability to blend the art of Indian design with the science of Silicon Valley scaling. We've been on an incredible journey so far, working hard to build a company that employees and customers love."*

To infinity and beyond: Building a product nation

"India's evolution into a product nation is inevitable," said Girish with characteristic conviction. "It's the natural next step for India's soft power evolution."

This confidence isn't unfounded. Girish drew parallels with India's IT Services success story, where homegrown giants like TCS, Infosys, and Wipro and global majors like IBM, Accenture, and Capgemini have thrived. This foundation has created something crucial: a vast pool of engineering talent ready to drive India's product revolution.

As Girish pointed out, "We have people working in those companies who have built global products. Then, we have companies like Freshworks, Flipkart, and Ola, where we have built B2C and B2B products. Our engineers know how to build truly world-class business and consumer software products."

Several factors are converging to make this vision a reality. India's emerging strength in AI and machine learning is particularly noteworthy. "India is the second largest contributor to AI/ML repositories on GitHub after China. US is third in the quantity of AI talent available," noted Girish.

This positions India favorably in the rapidly evolving AI landscape. But for Girish, the vision of India as a product nation goes beyond creating successful companies—it's about transforming India's entire economic landscape. It means creating high-quality jobs, developing valuable intellectual property, and positioning the country as a global leader in technology innovation.

Girish's commitment to this vision is perhaps best exemplified by SaaSBoomi. What began in 2015-16 as SaaSX—an unconference in Chennai with just 40 companies—has evolved into something much bigger.

Co-created with Avinash Raghava, who was then in the policy think tank iSPIRT, SaaSBoomi emerged from the recognition that India needed a SaaS ecosystem. What started as a small gathering of founders building global SaaS products from India has since become a cornerstone of India's SaaS ecosystem.

Girish noted the enthusiasm in smaller cities. "Not just the metros—when we do SaaSBoomi in tier 2 and 3 towns, you'll be amazed to see the number of founders who show up." This grassroots enthusiasm suggests that the product nation dream has the potential to drive economic development across all of India, not just in traditional tech hubs.

Looking ahead, Girish has an ambitious vision for Indian software products,

> ***"I think by 2030 we will be creating USD500 billion or USD 1 trillion worth of value. And maybe USD50 billion dollars of revenue."***

While he acknowledged that the exact numbers may vary, the trajectory is clear - India is poised for exponential growth in the SaaS and AI sectors, becoming a product nation.

"I think we are living the dream."

From product nation to sports nation: The FC Madras vision

Girish's commitment to building India's future extends beyond technology into sports through FC Madras, a football academy he established.

The genesis of this vision came from a simple observation: watching children play football on a dusty field in Chennai, while during his travels to the US, he'd see empty, well-maintained soccer fields.

"When I used to travel for work, I saw a very different scenario in the US, where the weather is cold, and soccer fields are empty. I'd often see a dad and kid just practicing scoring goals. They have the fields, but many days they don't have 22 players to fill them," he recalled. This disparity inspired him to invest around Rs 100 crore to build a world-class football facility in Mahabalipuram, near Chennai.

The academy operates with clear objectives—focusing on player development, international exposure, holistic programming, and creating a sustainable model.

Through FC Madras, Girish aims to address a fundamental challenge in Indian sports, "Academic kids like Sundar (Pichai) end up really successful because of the system, and they end up in Google, but sporting champions are successful in India in spite of the system because there is no infrastructure, no opportunity. Some of them will be academically brilliant, some will be sporting champions; we have to create an environment for both of them to succeed."

The Making of Freshworks: Shekhar Kirani Chronicles the Freshworks Story

We sat down with Shekhar Kirani, Partner at Accel and Freshworks' first institutional investor, for a rare look into the making of one of India's most successful SaaS companies. As an early backer who has watched Freshworks grow from its first pitch to its landmark IPO, Shekhar offers unique insights into Girish Mathrubootham's journey as a founder.

Having backed numerous successful SaaS companies, including BrowserStack, Zenoti, Chargebee, and Amagi, Shekhar brings a seasoned perspective to what makes exceptional founders stand out.

In this conversation, he shares what convinced him to bet on Girish, unpacks G's distinctive approach to building products and teams, and reveal the critical decisions that transformed Freshworks from a single-product startup into a global SaaS powerhouse. Read on!

Q. What standout qualities did you observe in Girish in the early days?

Girish was very ambitious and confident. This was evident early on when he won money at a Microsoft event (Shekhar is referring to Freshworks (then Freshdesk) winning the Microsoft Bizspark Startup Challenge in 2011). Instead of keeping it (the money), he put all that into content marketing because he understood that every dollar spent would result in profitable customer acquisition. He wasn't worried about running out of cash; he was confident that if he built a great product and business, it would succeed.

He would often say that if he didn't know something, he would talk to those who did or hire people who knew. He was very skilled at spotting talent. For example, when he met my executive assistant, he immediately recognized her efficiency and tried to hire her. He did the same to Accel's senior associate. I had to tell him to back off!

He always looked for high-quality individuals, not just to fill a role. He believed that if you find good people, you can always find a role for them that aligns with their passions. This was a core skill of his.

Another key aspect was his understanding of customers, including their psychology and online behaviour.

I'd say that he was one of the best in the industry. For example, while most companies had three pricing plans, he would implement five. He explained that the fifth plan was not designed to be widely purchased but to encourage customers to land on the fourth plan. He had studied it in detail and was able to get people to buy the specific plan that he wanted them to buy.

He was also a master of customer acquisition through search. He was very clear that search was the primary way to acquire customers. He constantly looked for what people were searching for, which keywords they were using, and where they were spending their time. He also recognized that each channel has limits in terms of how large it can become. When a channel became inefficient, he would open up new channels to continue to scale.

Q. Girish has always been known for his product management skills. What, in your opinion, makes him so good at it?

Many people think of a product as just the tool that customers use, but for Girish, the product is everything a customer touches. This includes emails, sales interactions, customer support responses, the website, the logo, how he was perceived at a conference, and even how he dressed.

He believed every interaction should make people feel good about the company. He was very particular about this aspect and also the UI/UX. He would constantly look for ways to improve it.

Q. What are your thoughts on how he built the organizational culture of Freshworks? Any standout memories/recollections?

At all-hands meetings, he would initially ask people what they thought the company should focus on. Later, he created an anonymous spreadsheet where people could ask questions and upvote them, with the top ten questions being answered. Despite concerns, he believed that even if there were tough questions, he should be able to answer them. This approach meant that his work and actions had to be transparent. He couldn't be arbitrary because people would challenge him. Any decision would be questioned, whether about hiring or salaries, so he had to provide clear answers.

He wanted everyone to have some form of equity and fought for small amounts of secondary offerings whenever possible so employees could see some monetary gain.

He was very employee-friendly, creating a family environment, or "Kutumb", as he called it. He was open to moving people between roles to help them find their niche. He cared about his people and supported them.

At their first annual event, 'Refresh', I vividly remember that a lot of women were winning the sales awards. I noted that 30-40% of the sales team were women, and they were doing exceptionally well. Girish explained that some had only worked for seven months due to maternity leave, but they were still exceeding their sales targets. He found that compassionate and motivated women who received training were phenomenal salespeople who truly cared about their customers. He ensured their safety and security, especially for night shifts, by providing food and other support. These were unique initiatives in the early days.

Q. All VCs look for founder-market fit. How did that play out in Girish's case? Obviously, he came with prior product-building and leadership experience, but building your own company is a totally different ballgame.

The 'founder market fit' for Girish and Freshworks was phenomenal. He initially focused on his strengths in the SMB and mid-market segments because he knew how to operate there. He started with inbound marketing and then added outbound. He began with Freshdesk and then added Freshservice, Freshsales, and other products.

His framework was always to focus first on his strengths. If those strengths aligned with a market opportunity, he would pursue it. He was honest about what he was good at and not good at. For example, he preferred to launch new products rather than go after the enterprise market (in the early years), which he felt he was not prepared for.

He was not a fan of spreadsheets, calling them 'MBA math', but I pushed him to use them for projections. He had never done it before, but once he did, he realised that hitting targets like 5 million ARR was possible. This helped him to see that by increasing spending and using multiple channels, he could achieve more growth. This shifted his view, and he started using projections and simple maths.

Q. How has your relationship with Girish evolved with the growth of the company? I guess there is also a certain emotional connection, as it was also your first-ever bet as an Accel VC.

The first set of investors is like an outsourced co-founder. They might not be in the same office, but you should feel free to call when in doubt. And if I (as an investor) have an idea, I should be able to contact the founder or the founding team and say, 'Hey, this is what I'm thinking about.' We are on the same side of the table.

As an early investor and a minority shareholder, I have responsibilities as a board member to the team and to align with the company's success, so transparency is key.

Girish would sign off on anything if I said so. But what I would do is explain it to him, and I earned my right to the trust. I'd let him know if something that I was asking would only be favouring me, and this is how it favours me, and this is the reason I need it from the Accel perspective versus this is how it may hurt Freshworks or you. Are you okay? He would think through and say, 'Okay, I'm fine, Shekhar.' There was no hidden agenda.

During the early days, founders don't know a lot about cap table, shareholder agreements, terms, etc.

But by the time later-stage investors show up, founders have also matured, and they have a good grasp of these terms. There is might in the company, there's a team in the company, and the protection of the company will be much higher.

The first few investors always have this special relationship because they work closely with the founders. The worst part is early investors not helping, that's when that relationship sours.

And I remember I used to tell him in the early days when there was a little bit of secondary, 'Girish, I've seen this many times: don't take too much of secondary; you're going to build a very large company. Just take money that is absolutely needed and maybe a little bit more for cushion.'

I told him, 'One day, you'll remember this'. A few weeks back, when I was at his house in the Bay area, we remembered that story. We did the math. He would have lost at least tens and tens of millions, a massive number (if he had gone through with the secondary in the early days). I learned from him, and now I'm encouraging a lot of other founders to take a small amount of money in secondary so that they don't worry about money anymore, they go all out for winning the game.

Over the years, I've pushed Girish hard on 'moments of truth'. These are key events that change the trajectory of a company. For example, I pushed Girish hard on AI in 2019 and 2020, urging him to hire people in the valley and turn the potential threat into an asset. He eventually did launch Freddy (Freshworks's AI agent) sooner than anyone else in India, but I was constantly pushing him on the topic of AI.

Q. What was Girish's mantra for hiring global talent? In India, especially with younger talent, we know how he operated. He'd see their potential and put them in roles where they had a natural inclination.

He initially used the same playbook that he knew in India but then realised that at the leadership level, smart people alone weren't enough. He realised he needed people with "muscle memory", meaning the experience of doing that kind of work. Then, he began hiring leaders with the right kind of experience. He would convince anyone if he knew they were the right person for the company.

Q. What makes Girish a great storyteller?

First, he has an 'elephant' memory. He remembers everything. Second, he's very good at making concepts understandable to the listener.

I think this skill came from when he used to teach Java. He started a teaching institute, and I believe he developed this skill there because he knew how to observe when students didn't understand and change his story accordingly. If his story doesn't land, he fixes it. He reads people very well, whether it's with investors, employees, leaders, customers or even in a keynote speech.

He's able to match his story to a specific audience. It's similar to what Jack Ma did at Alibaba, who was also an English teacher. This has made me think that teachers should consider entrepreneurship!

Chapter 3
From Commodities to Consumer King

How Harsh Mariwala Transformed Marico into a Global Juggernaut

Mumbai's Masjid Bunder is a place of dizzying frenzy—narrow roads, narrower pavements with scores of vendors, and endless streams of commuters filling the streets. It is just one stop away from the city's central railway station, Chhatrapati Shivaji Maharaj Terminus. Not to mention, it is close to the docks, too.

You get the drift: It is chaotic.

It is hardly the place one would associate with a world-class FMCG company, and yet it is.

Source: Masjid Bunder as imagined by ChatGPT.

Masjid Bunder was where everything began for Harsh Mariwala and Marico (a portmanteau of 'Mari'wala and 'co'mpany).

With household brands such as Parachute, Saffola, Nihar, and Revive, Marico is a unique Indian FMCG success story. In a market dominated by international giants, Marico has earned its rightful place as a leader in numerous categories.

Remarkably, this isn't just in India. Marico has successfully scaled Southeast Asia, the Middle East, and African countries, traditionally dominated by companies like Unilever and P&G.

However, Marico isn't the usual 'founder finds a problem, solves it and becomes big' story. It was, in a sense, centuries in the making.

Yes, you read it right.

Centuries.

Marico begins

All brands, like superheroes, have an origin story. And so does Marico.

Marico's journey began over a century ago, in 1872, when two brothers, Kanji and Vasanji Morarji, left their home in Kutch for Mumbai, where they established Kanji Khetsi & Co, a cotton trading business. Vasanji's son Vallabhdas—Harsh Mariwala's grandfather—was born in 1896, shortly before his father's untimely death.

The young Vallabhdas grew up under his uncle Kanjibai's wing, and in 1916, they shifted from cotton to spices from Kerala. Under the banner of Kanji Morarji, they flourished, eventually establishing a processing plant in the backwaters of Alleppey.

During the 1911 census, the British government assigned surnames to everyone. However, Kutchi families did not have surnames. Hence, Vallabhdas came to be known as 'Mariwala' due to his primary trade in pepper, which is *mari* in Gujarati.

Until independence, the British had an iron grip on trade and export. No Indian was given the right to export goods out of India. Post-independence, Vallabhdas truly began to 'spread his wings.' Together with his eldest son Charandas (Harsh's father), he built a reputation for exporting India's finest commodities to global markets.

1948 marked a turning point. Vallabhdas and Charandas consolidated their growing empire under Bombay Oil Industries Pvt. Ltd. (BOI). The company grew rapidly, establishing facilities across Kerala and Bombay—a crushing plant for coconut oil, an edible oil refinery, an oleochemicals plant, and a spice extraction unit.

As the business grew, Charandas brought his three brothers into the fold, each taking charge of crucial operations: Hansraj at Shree Jagdish Oil Mills in Porbandar, Jaisinh managing finances, and Kishore leading oleochemicals and spices. Under this collective leadership, BOI transformed from a trading business into a flourishing family enterprise.

Into this thriving enterprise, Harsh Mariwala was born in 1951. His childhood home, Kanmoor House (named after his great-uncle Kanji Morarji), doubled as BOI's headquarters on its fifth floor. Business wasn't just his heritage—it was quite literally home.

After completing his B.Com from Sydenham College, Harsh's request to pursue management studies abroad was met with a firm "no" from his father. But a casual trip to New York with a friend would change everything.

There, Harsh encountered a world where consumer brands dominated every aspect of life—from cosmetics to cookies, from hygiene to grooming. The contrast with India was stark: while American shelves burst with branded products, BOI's crown jewel, Parachute coconut oil, was still sold in industrial-sized tins like any other commodity.

Harsh formally joined BOI in 1971 and started traveling the length and breadth of the BOI empire to understand how things worked. He juggled everything from HR and improvisations in automation to managing information systems.

By the 1980s, four more third-generation Mariwalas had joined BOI, which meant there were nine Mariwalas (4 seniors, Harsh, and four more from the third generation). It was becoming all too apparent that BOI might not be able to handle the aspirations of them all.

The solution emerged after months of family deliberations: a demerger. On January 27, 1990, Harsh Mariwala separated from BOI with a clear vision: transforming a commodity-focused business into a modern consumer brands company. When he walked into the Kanmoor building on April 2, 1990, it wasn't as a scion of BOI but as the Managing Director of a new entity—Marico, ready to bring his consumer-first vision to life.

Today, Marico stands as a testament to Harsh's bold vision. The company has a turnover of over INR 9600 crores (USD 1.2 billion) in FY23-24, with a market capitalization of approximately INR 80,000 crore (USD 10 billion) as of December 2024, and employs close to 2000 people.

Marico touches the lives of 1 out of every 3 Indians through its portfolio of brands which are household names such as Parachute, Saffola, Hair & Care, Nihar Naturals, Mediker, Pure Sense, Coco Soul, Revive, Set Wet, Livon, Beardo, Just Herbs, True Elements and Plix.

But Marico's success story extends far beyond Indian borders. The company has established itself as a formidable player across Southeast Asia, the Middle East, and Africa, traditionally dominated by global FMCG giants. The international consumer products portfolio now contributes about 26% of the group's revenue.

How did a scion of a traditional trading family transform a commodity business into a world-beating FMCG behemoth? The answer lies in Harsh Mariwala's steely resolve to build his business intentionally, guided by the right principles. Here are the five most crucial lessons from his journey of transforming a centuries-old family-run business into an FMCG giant.

Lesson 1 - The winning formula: Know your strengths, hire for your weaknesses.

Every successful entrepreneur must find their own formula for success. For Harsh Mariwala, this meant first understanding what he was good at—and, more importantly, what he wasn't.

Even though he was from a traditional business family in the License Raj era, Harsh made a bold decision. While his peers were spending their time in Delhi's corridors of power, seeking licenses, considered the golden ticket to success, Harsh decided this wasn't his calling.

"For everybody else, the route to success was to get a license. It didn't appeal to me because I wasn't cut out for entertaining bureaucrats or making my way through the system to get licenses or favors," said Harsh.

Instead, Harsh found his sweet spot where his natural inclinations could shine—creating consumer brands in the edible oils business. "If I had gone into a business that wasn't based on what I liked, I wouldn't have succeeded," he reflected.

However, identifying his strengths was only half the battle. What truly set Harsh apart was his ability to confront his limitations head-on.

"When I started, as a commerce graduate, I didn't know what marketing was. I didn't know what distribution was. I wasn't able to attract talent," Harsh recalled.

His solution was ingenious.

Instead of letting his limitations hold him back, he turned to consultants who could teach him the ropes. "I worked with an HR professional from an MNC who spent evenings helping me with HR issues, from drafting appointment letters to setting up various systems." (Side note: Harsh might be among the first Indian leaders to prioritize the HR function. He wanted to bring as much science as possible into the art of hiring. It was a big shift from how Indian family-led businesses thought about talent.)

For marketing insights, he found a professor from IIM Ahmedabad, Labdhi Bhandari, who could only meet at night.

"Many times, I took evening flights, spent nearly the whole night discussing marketing with him, and returned the next morning," he recalled. "That's the adjustment and sacrifice needed to learn."

Perhaps most striking in Harsh's approach was his willingness to learn at every opportunity, including agencies that he hired. "The first thing I would tell ad agencies was, 'Okay, we're appointing you, but you have to teach me advertising.' I made up for my lack of knowledge by reading, attending short-term training programs, and interacting with thought leaders."

Harsh Mariwala
@hcmariwala
Follow

I firmly believe that our lives should be a perpetual journey of learning.

Whenever an opportunity arises, I seize it, whether through an interaction, observation, or by reading or listening.

Learning need not always be structured. For instance, during my daily workouts at the gym, I always listen to podcasts - this is my way of learning.

Similarly, when I'm travelling, it provides the perfect opportunity to read books.

While not every effort may result in learning, the intention to learn is what truly matters.

9:54 am · 13 Jun 24 · **4,586** Views

10 Reposts **1** Quote **54** Likes **1** Bookmark

Source: Harsh Mariwala's X (Formerly Twitter) Account

This commitment to learning paid off. When it came time to announce Marico to the world in April 1990, the press campaigns showed remarkable marketing savvy. Headlines like '200 Employees Walk Out of Bombay Oil' (announcing the transition to Marico) and 'Mass Killer Nabbed' (promoting 'good for heart' Saffola) demonstrated how quickly he had mastered the art of attention-grabbing advertising.

As the business grew, Harsh faced a crucial challenge: attracting top talent while operating from Mumbai's crowded Masjid Bunder area. "Half the time, good talent would just run away before coming to the office. So, how do you overcome that negativity? As an entrepreneur, you never say no, you need to try out some different approaches."

His creative solution? "We started inviting them to the Willingdon Club, close to where we lived. You meet once, meet twice, and then gradually explain that this is the office space for now, but it's temporary—we'll move out soon."

Looking at global giants for inspiration, Harsh set ambitious standards for talent acquisition. "My role models were companies like FMCG giants, Levers, Procter & Gamble, and L'Oreal. And they all had was good talent." This vision led to a realization that many entrepreneurs struggle to deal with.

> *"When you are small, you are doing things yourself. But when you become larger, you're getting things done. It's a big shift."*

Harsh wasn't threatened by hiring people more qualified than himself. "I wasn't qualified, yet I started recruiting talent more qualified than me, like MBAs and chartered accountants." But he ensured he could hold his own: "If I'm recruiting an MBA, then I better know what MBA concepts are and be able to talk to them."

Source: Harsh Mariwala's X (Formerly Twitter) Account

This powerful combination—clear self-awareness, relentless learning, and the courage to hire people smarter than himself—didn't just build a team. It laid the foundation for Marico's transformation from a family business into a global consumer giant.

Lesson 2 - You need to create a very strong right to win.

In the 1990s, competing with deep-pocketed FMCG giants seemed like a losing battle. While most Indian companies tried to challenge these multinationals head-on—and failed—Harsh Mariwala saw a different path to victory.

Instead of challenging the giants directly, he developed a

counter-intuitive strategy: identify categories the multinationals considered too small or insignificant, then dominate them completely by creating a strong right to win.

> *"Though we were in a similar space of FMCG, we didn't compete with many of the larger players because portfolio choice to me was very important. So, we selected portfolios where we had a very strong right to win and where we can become a market leader."*

The hair oils market exemplified this approach."Hair oils is not something which resonates with the MNCs. Hair oils business is bigger than shampoos. And we had a great opportunity to create a big hair oil market and become a market leader in that."

This selective approach extended to other categories. Take shampoos, for instance. Instead of competing in the mainstream market, Marico acquired a specific niche: "We compete in the anti-lice shampoo segment, which is much smaller than the main shampoo market. But we hold a 70% market share because, for MNCs, it doesn't make sense to focus on such a small category."

But Marico didn't just find niches—it created entirely new categories by solving problems that larger companies hadn't even recognized. The story of Revive, Marico's instant fabric starch, perfectly illustrates this innovative approach.

Harsh liked his cotton shirts starched. He noticed his wife's struggle with traditional starching—boiling water, mixing starch, and hoping for consistent results. The solution? Pre-gelatinized starch that dissolved instantly. This simple yet revolutionary product created an entirely new category where Marico could lead.

Perhaps the most sophisticated application of Marico's strategy came in commoditized markets. The Saffola story illustrates how to create the right to win through premium positioning in a commodity business.

"Edible oil is an extremely competitive segment, with very little product quality differentiation between brands. To achieve higher margins, you need a strong differentiator," Harsh explained.

Rather than competing on price, Marico positioned Saffola as a health brand. "At the time, safflower oil was associated with lowering cholesterol, so we positioned Saffola as a brand focused on heart health and cholesterol reduction." This positioning evolved strategically: "The brand transitioned from cholesterol reduction to heart health and now to a broader association with overall health."

The results were remarkable. Harsh said, "Saffola offers significantly higher margins, possibly the highest in the edible oil category, both in the country and globally, thanks to its health-focused positioning."

This commitment to market leadership required not just knowing where to win but also having the courage to walk away from categories where they could not dominate. When Marico's sunflower oil brand Sweekar showed no path to differentiation, they didn't hesitate to exit. "There's no differentiation, and gross margins in that business are only around

5%-10%. So we decided it was lowering our margin profile and chose to exit that market."

This disciplined focus on creating and maintaining a "right to win" in every category has proven remarkably successful. Harsh remarked, "If you look at our portfolio today, we have 20 brands; I think all brands are market leaders in their segments." Marico's principle to evaluate an opportunity remains the same today: don't fight giants in their territory; create new territories where you can become the giant.

Lesson 3 - Acquisition is a means to an end. It's not an end by itself.

While most companies chase headline-grabbing acquisitions that often destroy value, Harsh Mariwala saw M&As differently: as precise surgical tools to fill specific gaps in Marico's business. This philosophy has guided every acquisition in Marico's history, each serving a distinct strategic purpose.

Take the case of hair oil Nihar. Harsh explained, "We were relatively weak in East India compared to other regions. Nihar was a perfect fit, helping us improve our presence in East India and achieve a consolidated market share of over 60% in the coconut oil category."

He added, "Nihar was acquired for INR 200 crores. Now the brand is easily worth INR 5,000 crores if I sell it."

Then there's the story of Mediker, which showcases the power of identifying undervalued assets that align with your business strategy. "It was owned by Procter & Gamble and put up for sale, so we bid for it. I think we spent around INR 8 to 10 crores at the time. Today, that brand could easily fetch INR

500 to 1,000 crores if we sold it."

However, for Harsh, these value appreciation benefits are secondary to the strategic fit.

"I think acquisition is a means to an end. It's not an end by itself. Why do you want to acquire is more important."

When Marico set its sights on international markets, this same disciplined approach guided its expansion. "In some countries where we didn't see an organic opportunity to extend our product range, we considered entering through acquisitions." However, the acquisitions had to meet critical criteria: "They had to be in hair care or skincare and provide us with market leadership."

This disciplined approach led to several strategic wins:

- Egypt: Acquired Fiancée and HairCode, securing 50% of the post-wash hair care market
- South Africa: Built leadership in ethnic haircare through multiple acquisitions
- Vietnam: Established presence in the specialized male grooming segment

Each acquisition (domestic or international) served as a strategic entry point into a category. "On the back of that entry, we were able to expand our range of products and market share in these countries."

Lesson 4 - Remove escape buttons to build a stronger business.

Marico's international journey began with an intriguing discovery: their Parachute coconut oil was being smuggled into the Middle East, even when exports weren't permitted. This black market demand signaled a massive untapped opportunity.

When India liberalized in the 1990s, Marico could finally pursue these markets legally. While most Indian companies saw international expansion purely as a growth opportunity, Harsh had broader ambitions.

But turning these ambitions into reality proved challenging. Harsh quickly learned that international markets demanded more than just occasional attention.

"India is such a large market that Indian employees wouldn't get enough time to focus on smaller international markets. These markets had potential but were often neglected.

Harsh's solution was radical but simple: eliminate what he called "escape buttons"—any excuse that would let people avoid fully committing to international markets.

"Out of frustration, I decided that the Indian team would no longer handle international business. I hired a Vice President of International at the same level as a senior Indian executive. The business scale was small, and they had to grow it."

This decision—investing in senior leadership for what was then a small business—seemed extravagant to many. But it proved transformative for Marico.

"Removing escape buttons and having

good talent with time to look at opportunities helped us build a much stronger international base."

"We started visiting markets, identifying which ones we wanted to be in," Harsh explained. The team became proactive, even planting seeds with bankers and local communities about potential acquisitions.

Today's results validate Harsh's approach. International markets now contribute 26% of Marico's turnover, but more importantly, they've become engines of innovation and talent development. As Harsh reflected, "Many a time we try to optimize, saying, 'okay, let the same person do that'. But, that doesn't work out because it's a completely different ballgame."

Lesson 5 - The Organization's interest comes first

The true test of a leader often comes in moments of personal conflict. For Harsh Mariwala, two pivotal decisions demonstrate his unwavering commitment to putting the organization's interests first.

The first came in 1996 when family dynamics forced him to take Marico public. "I had to go public," Harsh recalled. "There were family differences regarding finances. And I had to buy out the family members."

With shares in escrow and a valuation higher than anticipated, Harsh faced losing control of the company if he couldn't arrange payment. Despite unfavorable market conditions and a low valuation multiple, he chose to go public rather than risk the company's future.

What seemed like a forced move proved transformative. The public listing brought enhanced visibility, improved corporate image, and better ability to attract talent. Over time, Marico transformed from being perceived as a "branded commodities company" to a "full-blooded FMCG company."

The second test came in 2014, after 24 years at the helm. Despite the common expectation in Indian family businesses that children would inherit leadership, Harsh made another unconventional choice. He stepped down as CEO and MD, making way for Saugata Gupta, who had served as India's CEO for a decade.

His guiding principle?

> *"Whenever there is a conflict between the organization's interest and any stakeholder's interest, whether it's a key employee or whether it is the promoter, the organization's interest comes first."*

This principle provided clarity in situations clouded by tradition and personal attachment. "My son is not stepping into my shoes, which is unheard of, at least in most Indian families," he noted. "But my principle is—If it is good for the organization, then I will do it."

When principles meet progress

In a career spanning over five decades (53 years in 2024, to be precise), Harsh Mariwala has built more than just a successful FMCG company—he's demonstrated how, by taking an intentional and principled approach to company building, David can defeat the FMCG Goliaths. And not just in India but globally.

It wasn't just about making the right choices at that moment in time—it was about building decision-making principles that would outlast any individual:

- In talent: Creating systems where talent trumped everything else
- In strategy: Developing clear criteria for market entry and exit
- In growth: Establishing guardrails for acquisition and expansion
- In governance: Setting precedents that put institution above individual

The result is a company that's uniquely Indian yet global, profitable yet principled, ambitious yet grounded. At 73, Harsh continues to shape Marico's journey, proving that when business decisions are guided by Dharma, success naturally follows.

Harsh Mariwala @hcmariwala · Jul 4, 2024

One thing I like to do is regularly go on visits to stores and meet with the retailers and distributors.

It gives me a clear insight into the consumer mind and the emerging trends. Here I am at Shivraj Super Market in Parel, Mumbai.

How do you like to do consumer insighting

Show more

Empowering India's Changemakers

ASCENT Foundation

Founded in 2012 by Harsh Mariwala, ASCENT Foundation is a not-for-profit initiative designed to empower growth-stage entrepreneurs in India through the "Power of the Collective." It facilitates peer-to-peer learning via 'Trust Groups,' where non-competing entrepreneurs exchange experiences and insights in a confidential setting to learn from each other and foster personal growth.

"I believe entrepreneurs will drive India's growth story. It's their entrepreneurial spirit that will help us become a USD 10 trillion economy. Many entrepreneurs have great ideas but struggle with execution and scaling. Suppose I can help create a peer-to-peer learning platform where they can learn from each other. In that case, it will add value to their businesses, foster larger enterprises, contribute to India's growth, and generate employment."

As of 2024, ASCENT supports over 1,000 entrepreneurs with a cumulative turnover exceeding ₹1 lakh crore and has expanded from Mumbai and Chennai to Delhi, with aspirations to be present across India.

Marico Innovation Foundation

Established in 2003 by Harsh Mariwala, the Marico Innovation Foundation (MIF) is a philanthropic entity dedicated to fostering innovation across India's business and social sectors. MIF operates several core programs:

- Scale-Up Program: Provides bespoke, no-equity acceleration support to for-profit startups with annual revenues between ₹ one crore and ₹100 crore.
- Innovation for India Awards: A biennial event recognizing breakthrough Indian innovations that have positively impacted society.

Through these initiatives and others, MIF aims to create a robust innovation ecosystem, driving large-scale socio-economic and environmental impact across the nation.

Chapter 4
Nice Guys Win Big

Anand Deshpande's Contrarian Playbook to Build Generational Companies

"Nice guys finish last," goes the cynical maxim of corporate ambition.

Anand Deshpande, the founder and Chairman of Pune-based Persistent Systems, would vehemently disagree.

Starting with just \$21,000 and armed with a PhD's methodical mindset, Anand built an \$11 billion technology juggernaut—all while remaining, methodically and profitably, nice.

His origin story reads like an antidote to Silicon Valley mythology. At Campion School, Bhopal, he wasn't the precocious wunderkind disrupting classroom norms, but rather 'regular, disciplined, diligent, and someone who completed homework daily.'

At IIT Kharagpur, where India's brightest minds converged, he distinguished himself through the same methodical work ethic—a trait that would become his signature in business.

Consider how he tackled the challenge of US university applications. While his IIT-Kharagpur classmates focused on individual applications, Anand saw a system waiting to be optimized. With sixteen peers pursuing foreign universities, he identified a subtle flaw in their approach: professors writing multiple recommendations to the same institutions would inevitably dilute each letter's impact.

His solution was characteristically methodical. He 'orchestrated' a coordinated effort, creating a detailed chart of target universities to ensure no overlap in professorial recommendations. The result? Nearly every student secured coveted scholarships, and Anand himself had his pick of universities, eventually choosing Indiana University Bloomington.

This deep intellectual curiosity and systematic problem-solving would later become his north star, leading him to create one of India's earliest product engineering companies while others chased the well-worn path of IT services. But Anand's true genius lay not in building something different but in his ability to keep reinventing it.

At the core of Anand Deshpande's business approach is the philosophy of 'S-shaped curves,' which he has successfully applied to Persistent Systems over the last three and half decades.

The philosophy found an elegant expression in a 2019 conversation between Anand and chess grandmaster Vishwanathan Anand.

Anand hosted Vishwanathan Anand to talk about success. During the interaction, Anand asked his guest: "How does one stay motivated after achieving so much?" The chess legend's response was revealing: "There is a tendency to stick with what works, but everything has an expiry date, in a way that I cannot explain."

Everything has an expiry date!

That's exactly what S-curves represent—the inevitability of

stagnation unless one reinvents.

Anand has lived this truth. Under his leadership, Persistent Systems has navigated six distinct orbits, each demanding reinvention. "Every orbit has been unique," he explained.

> *"What works in one orbit rarely works in the next. What you do, how you behave, what team you need—all of these change. Each orbit has its own nuances and idiosyncrasies."*

These orbits—and the lessons they contain about persistent reinvention—form the chapters of Anand's playbook for building an enduring technology company.

Let's explore it together.

Lesson 1 - Be a persistent contrarian

In the Indian IT industry of the 1990s, conventional wisdom had a clear playbook: build large teams, optimize for scale, and chase every opportunity. Most founders followed this path. Anand Deshpande saw a different possibility—one that would combine methodical execution with contrarian thinking to achieve market leadership.

Persistent Systems began as an expression of Anand's methodical nature. While others chased scale, Anand built a company that would be unabashedly geeky, writing code not because they had to but because they loved to do it.

Anand explained Persistent's early days through his elegant framework of orbits. "In the first orbit, companies start with founders and their energy and passion. Your job is to do what comes your way. You're trying to find product-market fit. You have to respond to the situation and do what it takes," he shared.

"I had a database background, and we were working with Silicon Valley data product companies, building product engineering work for them, but not necessarily knowing that we were doing product engineering," Anand recalled of Persistent's first orbit, which lasted for the first 10 years of its existence, from 1990 to 2000.

The company remained deliberately focused—just 100 people with six PhDs—maintaining an enviable 35% profit margin. They weren't trying to be everything to everyone; they were computer science geeks doing what they did best.

The dot-com bust of 2001 forced a moment of reckoning. While other Indian IT companies pivoted their Y2K teams to general IT services, Persistent faced an existential challenge—they had never touched Y2K work.

"I just felt it was below my dignity to work on Y2K projects," Anand admitted with characteristic frankness.

The crisis marked a crucial evolution in Anand's methodical contrarianism. "By the time you come to the second orbit, you know you'll not die easily. You have a product. You're selling some things, but you (the founder) have maxed out. Now you have to shift gears and find the market where you can be a leader."

This is exactly what Persistent did. When everyone else said "IT this, IT that," they methodically built an entirely new category: Outsourced Product Development (OPD). But, mind you, this wasn't just clever marketing; it represented a fundamentally different approach to software development.

"We differentiated by defining it differently, saying that in an IT project, you have well-defined requirements and you do trade-offs between time and money. But in a product, the first thing you decide is when you want to ship the product. Then you decide how much you want to spend and you build the best possible product within the time and money." This fundamental difference in approach meant Persistent could speak the language of product teams, not IT departments.

The genius of this positioning lay in how it merged Anand's three core principles: methodical execution, contrarian thinking, and focused market leadership. While IT giants couldn't brand themselves as pure product engineering companies without compromising their larger businesses, Persistent could proudly claim leadership in OPD because "that's all we do." This systematic approach to choosing and dominating a specific market would become their defining advantage.

They doubled down on this identity in ways that often seemed counterintuitive to the traditional IT services playbook. They hired only computer science graduates, focused on programming rather than analysis, and targeted VPs of Engineering instead of CIOs. "We said we are geeks, we will roll our sleeves and write code with you," Deshapnde remembered.

While other companies rushed to build large sales teams in the US, Persistent didn't file their first H1B visa for a salesperson until 2003, thirteen years into the company's journey. This wasn't just frugality—it was a deliberate choice to build market leadership through technical excellence rather than sales muscle.

Persistent's methodical approach to defining and dominating a market niche reveals Anand's deeper insight into business success.

> ***"In any market," he remarked, "there can be only three leaders—they typically get 70% of the market share and dominate the market; everyone else gets the rest. So for any business to be successful and really benefit from the market and the tailwinds, you really need to become a leader; you need to be in the top three."***

His advice to companies is characteristically precise: "Be very clear about what is the market that you think you can win in, that you can dominate to establish a leadership position... If you are doing a $20 million business and you aspire to be $50 million, you need to be clear about what is that $250 million market where you can grab a 20% market share."

This is perhaps the most powerful lesson from Persistent's journey—being contrarian isn't enough, and being methodical isn't sufficient. True success comes from systematically identifying and dominating markets where your contrarian approach gives you an unassailable advantage. Everything else, as Anand learned, is just noise.

Lesson 2 - Think of customers as people and not companies

For Anand Deshpande, the importance of personal relationships wasn't a crisis-born insight—it was woven into his DNA. Even as a PhD student, he understood the power of genuine connections. "I learned many things, but also I was able to network quite a bit while I was in a PhD program," he recalled. "As a student, you get a chance to meet advisors, advisor's friends, and other people. I really built a good network during that period."

These relationships laid the foundation for Persistent's first contracts. "My first two contracts came from personal relationships," Anand shared. "One was with a friend in Bloomington in Indiana... Another was with O2 Technologies... I had met the founder Francois at a conference in Austin when I was a student."

During the dot-com bust of 2000, this people-first approach would prove its true strategic value.

While most companies frantically chased new business in a contracting market, a conversation with Ravi Venkatesan, an Indian business leader and former Chairman of Microsoft India, helped crystallize Persistent's contrarian path forward.

"Going after new customers right now, you'll not get them, but you'll lose your old ones as well," Venkatesan advised. This prompted Anand to rethink customer relationships fundamentally.

"Instead of thinking about customers as

companies, I think about customers as people in the company and work with them until the end," he reflected.

This wasn't just relationship management. Persistent doubled down on supporting their customers through their toughest times working with them in the trenches. "A little counterintuitive," Anand admitted, "but it really helped us a lot."

The strategy proved transformative. When the market eventually recovered, these relationships became Persistent's greatest asset. "All the people I worked with at that point, they felt like we lived with them," he recalled. "So when they moved to other companies, they took us along with them."

This lesson proved so valuable that when the 2008 financial crisis hit, Anand didn't just dust off this playbook—he amplified it. When customers started asking for discounts, he saw another opportunity for relationship building. His team was instructed not to give discounts without CEO meetings.

These crisis-prompted meetings with 150 CEOs not only helped preserve business during the downturn but opened up entirely new strategic possibilities for Persistent. (More on this in the next section).

What began as methodical relationship-building in graduate school evolved into a powerful strategic framework: in technology services, true differentiation comes not from technical excellence alone but from the depth of relationships with people during their toughest moments. This insight would prove crucial as Persistent prepared to enter its next orbit, which would take them directly to the CEO's office.

Lesson 3 - Do what the CEO cares about

While the company was experiencing a tough time during the 2008 Global Financial Crisis, Anand powered his way into the offices of 150+ CEOs for contract renewal negotiations, conducting an ethnographic study of the CEO's mind at scale.

What emerged was more than just market intelligence—it was a detailed cognitive map of how CEOs operate. "What I found very interesting, was that CEOs think very differently from non-CEOs," Anand observed, crystallizing his findings into what would become Persistent's strategic north star.

He identified three distinct patterns in the CEO's mindset.

1. The Priority List: Despite overseeing vast enterprises, CEOs maintain an almost maniacal focus on just 5-7 key initiatives. Everything else—no matter how vital to operations—is delegated.
2. Revenue Obsession: "No CEO will say they don't care about the top line. Everyone needs new business. That is the number one priority," Anand noted. This singular focus on growth transcended industry, geography, and even market conditions.
3. The Network Imperative: Perhaps most counter-intuitively, CEOs revealed themselves as compulsive connectors. "CEOs want to network and are willing to make introductions and meet people just for the heck of it. Even if it may or may not help the business directly," Anand observed. "They are willing to make introductions with no immediate payoff." For them,

> it wasn't mere socializing—it was about building relationships that might bear fruit in unexpected ways.

The mismatch between Persistent's ambition and its business model hit hard. Anand recalled, "At that time, our customer was VP Engineering or CTOs, not CEOs. CEOs didn't know what we were doing for them. Go to them and say, Oh, yeah. It's great to know that you guys are working with us and yeah, VP Engineering, John is taking care of you."

This insight catalyzed Persistent's transition to the third orbit—from a pure product engineering company to what Anand termed as "everything around the product." Persistent started doing everything around the product, such as deployment, customer engagement, market intelligence, and strategic consulting.

This shift proved transformative.

Today, Persistent's evolution from a pure engineering shop to a full-service digital partner stands as a testament to the power of speaking the CEO's language.

"The product engineering work, while it's very important and critical, the CEO doesn't care about it," Anand reflected.

"We'll do whatever the CEO cares about. That was very valuable and I found it very useful."

Lesson 4 - Timing is everything

In business, being right isn't enough—you have to be right at the right time. Anand Deshpande's journey offers deep insights into knowing not just what to do but when to do it.

Three inflection points shaped Persistent's journey.

The first was the Intel Capital investment in 2000. While peers chased large funding rounds during the dot-com boom, Persistent chose a different path. They traded just 3.5% equity for $1 million—a modest sum that valued the 125-person company at $20 million. But Anand wasn't playing a valuation game; he was buying credibility at exactly the right moment.

The timing proved prescient. As Persistent entered its second orbit—the phase where they needed to establish market leadership—the Intel association opened doors that would have taken years to crack otherwise.

"We got a good branding because of that. We became part of the Intel portfolio. Intel had a lot of companies in their portfolio, so we got to meet a lot of companies. We will attend their events where we could meet customers and partners," noted Anand.

The second strategic timing decision came in 2005, as Persistent prepared to scale its OPD leadership. Rather than chase the highest valuation, Anand sought investors who could strengthen their US presence. "I was trying to recruit more in the US," he explained, "and I thought having someone who was US-based who could be part of the board and the company would be good." So they brought legendary investors Promod Haque (Norwest) and Navin Chaddha (Gabriel Venture Partners) on board, raising $20 million at a $100 million valuation.

However, the most telling example of Anand's timing instincts came with their IPO journey. In 2008, with papers filed and ready, Persistent watched markets deteriorate daily. "Every time I would go to Mumbai, the listing price would decrease by 10%." Instead of pushing through, they pulled back—a decision that seemed overly cautious at the time.

This patience paid off spectacularly. When Persistent finally went public in 2010, it became the first company to IPO after the global financial crisis. The offering was oversubscribed 93 times, setting the stage for remarkable long-term value creation. "From that point onwards, our stock appreciation has been more than Google's stock appreciation," added Anand.

Even Anand's personal transition from CEO to Chairman in 2019 exemplifies this timing acumen. The move, made just before COVID-19, allowed a fresh team under CEO Sandeep Kalra to guide Persistent through the pandemic, achieving 35% growth for two consecutive years. "I must not take much credit for it," Anand reflected. "I was involved in it all through, but the CEO and the team actually grew the business."

These weren't just lucky breaks—they were calculated decisions that recognized a fundamental business truth: the right move at the wrong time is still the wrong move. Each transition aligned perfectly with Persistent's orbit changes, demonstrating how strategic timing can transform good decisions into watershed moments.

Lesson 5 - Learn the art of strategic delegation

For most founders, letting go is the hardest part of scaling.

The very qualities that make entrepreneurs successful—passionate ownership, attention to detail, hands-on leadership—can become obstacles to growth.

Anand explained this paradox:

> *"When you are a founder-driven company, everyone works for the founder. It's the founder's mission and vision. But when you reach the second orbit, everyone needs to work for the company. The founder also must work for the company, and it's the company's vision and mission."*

This transition from "my company" to "our company" represents perhaps the most crucial evolution in a founder's journey. Many founders struggle with this shift, but Anand approached it with his characteristic methodical mindset.

His philosophy was radically meritocratic: "You should be the CEO of the company as long as you're the best person to be the CEO of the company, not because you're the founder."

This shaped Persistent's governance evolution. "By the time you get to the second orbit," Anand shared, "you want to have a governance structure, a board, and independent directors. These become crucial as you scale."

When it was time for his own transition from CEO to Chairman, Anand spent considerable time studying successful transitions, particularly in the IT industry. "I spent a lot of time talking to other CEOs and founders who had made that transition," he recalled. "And in the IT industry, I'm sort of the one-and-a-half second generation, and so many of the senior people who run companies, I met them and learned how to make the transition happen."

One piece of advice stood out, "You should have enough other things to do; otherwise, you'll keep interfering." This insight proved crucial. Rather than hovering over the new management, Anand channeled his energy into other initiatives: teaching entrepreneurship through his Second Orbit program, building the deAsra Foundation to support nano-entrepreneurs, and working on healthcare initiatives like the India Cancer Genome Atlas.

This wasn't just about keeping busy but about finding ways to scale impact beyond direct management. Just as Anand had learned to delegate operational responsibilities within Persistent, he was now learning to delegate the company's leadership.

Perhaps most tellingly, Anand now spends significant time teaching other entrepreneurs through his Second Orbit program, helping them navigate their own transitions from founder-driven to professionally managed companies.

This journey from founder to enabler offers a powerful lesson for entrepreneurs: true scale comes not from what you can do yourself but from what you can empower others to achieve.

Being persistent

When Anand Deshpande returned to India in October 1990, he faced insurmountable odds. India's software exports barely registered globally, infrastructure was primitive, and the license raj still throttled entrepreneurial ambition.

"India was in a pretty sad situation at that point. It was very hard to imagine what Indian IT can become," he recalled. The challenges were both systemic and specific: a two-year wait for a telephone line, software exports totaling less than $100 million nationally, and import duties that made accessing basic technology prohibitively expensive.

Yet these constraints would prove oddly advantageous. Anand recognized that building a company in such an environment would forge capabilities that would be hard to replicate in more mature markets.

The numbers tell a compelling story of transformation: from a small database engineering shop to a top-line of $1.19 billion (FY 24); from a team of 100 to over 23,800 employees across 21 countries; from India's pre-liberalization struggles to 268% growth since 2020.

But the real story lies in how this transformation was achieved. Each of Persistent's six orbits represented not just a company evolving but a deliberate choice to persist through often painful transformations rather than settle for incremental growth. From the early days when they proudly declared, 'We are geeks, we roll our sleeves, we write code with you' to their current stature as a digital transformation partner for global enterprises, the company has maintained its core identity while continuously reinventing its capabilities.

In many ways, Persistent's journey mirrors India's evolution from a technological backwater to a global IT powerhouse. But while many factors drove India's transformation, Persistent's growth came from a singular quality that Anand considers fundamental to success.

When asked about the most important quality in a winner,

his answer is characteristically precise: "Persistence."

In an industry obsessed with disruption, Persistent's story offers a different narrative—one of methodical evolution, strategic patience, and unwavering focus on fundamentals. While others chased quick wins, Anand built for permanence, creating not just a successful company but a template for sustainable growth in the technology sector. As India enters its next phase of technological leadership, Persistent's journey from a small Pune-based startup to a global digital engineering leader serves as a reminder that in the end, it's not the fastest or the loudest who wins—it's the most persistent.

Persistent Systems' Orbits

First Orbit: The bootstrap phase focused on database engineering for Silicon Valley products. The company grew to 100 people with 35% profit margins and a small but highly specialized team of computer science experts.

Second Orbit: Created and dominated the Outsourced Product Development (OPD) category, differentiating from IT services by focusing purely on product engineering and establishing market leadership.

Third Orbit: Expanded beyond pure engineering to full product lifecycle services after Anand's strategic meetings with 150 CEOs during the financial crisis, shifting from serving just VPs of Engineering to engaging with CEOs.

Fourth Orbit: Leveraged their product engineering expertise to help traditional businesses become software-driven companies, riding the "software is eating the world" wave.

Fifth Orbit: Marked by Anand's transition from CEO to Chairman, coinciding with COVID-19, leading to two consecutive years of 35% growth under new leadership.

Sixth Orbit: Currently a ~$1.19 billion revenue company evolving into digital engineering while maintaining its core DNA of engineering excellence, with a 40-60 split between pure product companies and enterprises needing product-like software.

About deAsra Foundation

The deAsra Foundation, established in 2013 by Anand Deshpande and his family, addresses one of India's most pressing challenges: large-scale job creation. The foundation's name combines 'D' for Deshpande with 'ASRA'—representing the initials of Anand, Sonali, Rhea, and Arul, reflecting the family's collective vision.

deAsra focuses on empowering "nano entrepreneurs"—small businesses with revenues between ₹5 lakhs and ₹1 crore. These businesses form the backbone of India's economy, with 98% of enterprises employing fewer than 20 people and 95% generating less than ₹1 crore in revenue. Small businesses contribute to 70% of India's employment, making their success crucial for economic growth.

To tackle this, deAsra has developed a systematic, tech-enabled platform that addresses five key challenges for entrepreneurs:

1. Access to Capital/Credit
2. Access to Markets
3. Access to Technology
4. Access to Teams/Talent
5. Compliance Support

With over 300,000 entrepreneurs already in its network, deAsra aims to onboard 10 million businesses in the coming years. It is building systems to support half a million new businesses annually and has partnered with organizations like the Army Wife Welfare Association (AWWA) and Swadeshi Jagaran Manch's Swavlambi Bharat Abhiyan to create a robust nationwide support ecosystem for grassroots entrepreneurs. As Anand explains, "India needs 16 to 18 million new jobs every year, and real jobs happen when people find employment for themselves. For that, we need job creators." Through deAsra, he envisions a future where millions of small businesses thrive, driving employment and economic prosperity across India.

Chapter 5
From India to the World

The Hardware Revolution Led by GreyOrange and Ultrahuman

They say that the road to success is not a straight line. For Akash Gupta, this 'road' would lead through college robotics labs, while for Mohit, it went through a Thailand-based martial arts camp called Tiger Muay Thai, ultimately converging on a shared destination: building best-in-class hardware companies from India for the world.

By his early twenties, Akash had more stamps in his passport than most seasoned executives, traveling the world for robotics competitions with his BITS-Pilani senior and future co-founder, Samay Kohli. As part of team AcYut, a humanoid robot they developed in the early 2010s, they were at the forefront of the humanoid robotics wave, captivating engineering circles.

But more than the glamor of traveling the world, Akash was enamored by the joy of bringing textbook concepts to life through hardware. What started with tinkering with DC motors and access to a college CNC machine would eventually reshape global warehouse automation.

Meanwhile, Mohit Kumar was charting a different course. After riding the adrenaline rush of food tech as the founder of

Runnr (a Blume Fund II portfolio company later acquired by Zomato), a detour to Thailand's Tiger Muay Thai sparked a deep interest in tracking his health. What began as a personal quest would soon evolve into a mission to revolutionize health tracking for millions globally.

When Akash launched GreyOrange (Blume Fund I vintage) in 2011, "deep tech" wasn't even part of the startup lexicon. The idea of building industrial robots in India—where even basic hardware manufacturing was a challenge—seemed almost delusional. Yet today, GreyOrange has deployed over 15,000 robots worldwide, orchestrating operations for retail giants like Walmart, Nike, and H&M in the US, proving that world-class robotics innovation can emerge from anywhere.

Mohit's vision for Ultrahuman (Blume Fund III) was equally audacious. Launched amid the global pandemic, the company chose to compete with tech giants hundreds of times its size. Their flagship product, the Ultrahuman Ring AIR, now sells in 150 countries, going toe-to-toe with global leaders in health tracking. In a testament to their global ambitions, they're even setting up manufacturing operations in the US to serve the American market better.

The success of GreyOrange and Ultrahuman exemplifies that with the right vision and relentless execution, hardware companies from India can not just compete but win on the global stage. If you are a founder already on a journey to sell globally or about to start one, you will find these lessons invaluable. Let's dive in.

Lesson 1 - Early stage hardware companies should

own their core manufacturing

In the early days of GreyOrange, Akash faced a decision that would define their journey. They had raised a small round of INR 50 lakhs (approx $100,000 then) but weren't sure if they should get a CNC machine in-house—it would cost them half their funds. "We needed rapid prototyping capabilities," Akash recalled, "but Gurgaon's manufacturing ecosystem was built only for car manufacturing. No one would touch small batches for a startup." They took the punt and bought the machine.

What seemed like a constraint—India's lack of hardware infrastructure in 2012—became their competitive advantage. By bringing manufacturing in-house, GreyOrange gained something more valuable than cost savings: the ability to iterate rapidly and maintain complete control over its product development, crucial for a company still searching for product-market fit.

Ultrahuman's journey echoes this philosophy, albeit catalyzed by different circumstances. When COVID disrupted global supply chains in 2022, Mohit and his team decided not to let a crisis go to waste. They realized the strategic importance of data access in health technology and decided to "verticalize heavily and control the entire end-to-end experience."

As Mohit explained,

> *"We had heard of horror stories where everything was ready and the factory in China just shut down. So, people can't really take the goods away from it. So*

> *because of all of these things, as a forcing function, we decided that if we have to control our future, evolve the product, launch new products in the future, we have to do it ourselves. There's no other answer. Maybe it's the harder answer. But we have to learn the laws of physics and understand how does it really work."*

The advantages of building in-house are evident in both companies' trajectories.

When Ultrahuman began producing rings with mirror-finished surfaces, local vendors—accustomed to industrial components—couldn't grasp the need for such a high-quality finish. For GreyOrange, in-house capabilities proved crucial when they needed to scale from three sortation systems to 47 in just six months for Flipkart's Big Billion Day—a feat almost impossible with external vendors alone.

Building in-house created a second-order benefit: deep product expertise. Instead of merely assembling components, teams developed intimate knowledge of every aspect of their products—knowledge that proved invaluable for innovation. While this path demanded significant upfront investment and patience in training fresh graduates, it created a culture of deep technical understanding that outsourcing could never replicate.

These skills now permeate the organization's DNA, creating long-term benefits. As Akash noted, "We still assemble our own robotic technology in-house. We do a lot of third-party manufacturing and sources as well, but our core robotic technology, we still assemble a lot in our Gurgaon plant."

To be sure, the lesson isn't about maintaining everything in-house forever; both companies eventually developed vendor networks and partnerships. Rather, it's about recognizing that while the temptation to outsource everything in the early days might be strong, building core capabilities in-house—even if it means starting smaller or moving slower—is crucial for long-term success.

Lesson 2 - Scale comes from winning global markets

The journeys of GreyOrange and Ultrahuman reveal a crucial insight: the path to building a large hardware company inevitably runs through global markets. Both companies discovered this early in their journeys.

For GreyOrange, the realization came naturally. They had saturated the local market, "There was nobody left to sell sortation systems in India," Akash recalled. This realization, combined with their ambition to work with Fortune 100 brands, pushed them to look beyond borders. Their journey began with Japan, where they learned their first lessons about global standards.

"I remember we shipped the first batch of 70 robots to one of the customers in Japan. In Japan they do a white room analysis where they keep the bot in white light and look at it from different angles. Soon we received a long email with pictures of our

bots with details like, 'here is a scratch,' 'this bot head seems to be a little bit damaged,' and more. That almost forced us to raise our manufacturing standards to match their requirements," recalled Akash.

However, the real inflection point came with their decisive pivot to the US market through an exclusive partnership with GXO Logistics. "We grew 10 times in three years in the US, compared to what India and Asia did in seven years," said Akash.

Ultrahuman took a different but equally ambitious approach to global expansion. They realized this during a team meeting in 2022 when they were projecting growth trajectories. The math was simple: staying focused on a few markets would make the path to becoming a billion-dollar company unnecessarily long.

"We were looking at some projections. In the next six years, this is where we will reach, and this is what the category will be. And I think one of our team members just said, 'look, I should turn pretty old by the time we'll do a billion dollars in revenue. That doesn't sound like a good plan'," remembered Mohit.

That conversation sparked a bold decision: go all out on global distribution, with just two guardrails—no performance marketing and profitability on every transaction. Today, Ultrahuman ships to 150 countries across 23 languages, and sells through major retailers like Walmart, Costco, and Best Buy in the US.

As Mohit said, "If it's a good product, every country, every consumer should want it."

The success of both companies reveals a lesson for founders: Start in India and scale globally to become a billion-dollar enterprise.

Lesson 3 - Great hardware companies need teams that see beyond the obvious

Building a pioneering hardware company requires more than just technical talent. It demands a team that can envision and create entirely new categories.

For GreyOrange, this journey began with what Akash calls "shared dreaming." "The only magic trick is spending an enormous amount of time with that first group of 20 people," he recalled.

Between 2012 and 2015, the founding team spent countless hours tinkering, dreaming, and discussing failures and aspirations. Back then, running a US warehouse with 1,000 bots seemed like the ultimate goal—today, that's just the beginning.

The evolution of the team at GreyOrange followed three distinct phases.

First came building a core group deeply connected to the vision, often working with fresh graduates willing to take risks on an ambitious hardware startup instead of seasoned professionals hesitant to join a 'strange' robotics startup in India.

The second phase involved integrating experienced talent while preserving the original culture. The third phase, triggered by global expansion, brought the challenge of managing teams across geographies while maintaining a unified vision.

"I remember when we first formally shifted out HQ from Gurgaon to Singapore and then to Atlanta, there was a lot of talk about decisions being taken out of Atlanta and what does that mean for folks in India," recounted Akash.

Akash said the founder has to solve this tension, but there are no easy solutions. He recalled, "I remember between 2018 to 2020, just before the pandemic hit, I was religiously doing 15 days India, 15 days US, because I wanted my India team to be very connected to what's happening in the US."

Ultrahuman took an equally deliberate approach to team building but with a different focus. They prioritized two traits: candidates had to be natural users of their product and could handle conflicts constructively, prioritizing solutions over arguments.

"We would ask questions like, 'if you have a delayed Indigo flight, what would you do about it?' And some people would say like, I'll go to Twitter and I'll rant about it'. We said. 'look, things are going to go bad in life and you've got to solve it'. You want optimism in life because you want to show up every day and win. We prioritize more optimistic people. I know that that could be a problem sometimes because of delusion and other issues. But then this is a bias that we have," said Mohit.

Mohit divides the hardware talent landscape in India into three layers: firmware development (where India has just 1% of the needed capacity), production engineering (which requires massive mindset shifts), and supply chain logistics (where capability has significantly improved). The real challenge is finding people who understand the pace and quality demands of modern hardware companies.

Akash agreed with Mohit's assessment, adding an anecdote from GreyOrange's early days.

> *"We were releasing a new version every 18 months and our teams, who were from car industry would say, 'Sir, in three years, even a prototype isn't possible. You are talking about a version release every 18 months.' This is because they are used to a 10-year upgrade cycle."*

This mindset gap between traditional hardware and startup thinking remains one of the biggest challenges for hardware innovation. But it's also where the opportunity lies. Successful companies build teams that see beyond conventional wisdom—teams that can re-imagine not just products but the very way hardware companies should operate. GreyOrange and Ultrahuman have shown that building category-defining products requires category-defying teams.

Lesson 4 - Move fast without breaking things (literally)

Building hardware companies demands a unique balance: combining software's rapid iteration with hardware's unforgiving nature. The journeys of GreyOrange and Ultrahuman reveal how to strike this balance.

A common pitfall in hardware development is overthinking and seeking perfection before launch. "Stop overthinking.

It's not as hard as it looks," advised Akash Gupta.

This might seem counterintuitive for hardware products, where you can't just push an update. Yet both founders insist that rapid iteration becomes even more crucial precisely because the stakes are higher. As Akash pointed out, "If you put 10,000 bots out in the market and have to do a recall, that's something that you really will have to think about whether you survive or not."

So what's the solution? Instead of spending all the time perfecting the product before launch, find the right early customers and be transparent about the product's development stage. The key is being "super transparent" about where you are in the journey. Both companies discovered plenty of customers willing to innovate alongside them. This approach enables real-world testing that no lab work can match.

Beyond finding the right customers, a technical mindset is crucial. Mohit stressed the importance of founders understanding the technical aspects deeply, even if they don't code themselves.

> *"If we don't understand technology, then we are just businessmen selling technology," he emphasized.*

This becomes crucial in hardware companies, where mechanical, electronic, and software components must work in perfect harmony.

Success in hardware demands thinking beyond local boundaries. As Akash pointed out, "Building a hardware startup out of India doesn't mean you got to source everything from India." This global perspective needs to be baked into the company's DNA from the beginning, whether it's about manufacturing locations, component sourcing, or market selection.

Perhaps the most difficult part is for hardware founders to balance two seemingly contradictory mindsets: the urgency to get products into users' hands quickly and the patience to build sustainable, scalable solutions. While software companies can push frequent updates, hardware companies must get more things right before shipping—yet they can't wait for perfection. GreyOrange and Ultrahuman have mastered this tightrope walk, proving it's possible to move fast without breaking things—literally.

Lesson 5 - Sell solutions not specifications

Hardware founders often fall in love with their technology. But the most successful ones understand a fundamental truth: customers don't really care about the technology—they care about what it helps them achieve. GreyOrange learned this lesson early.

Akash Gupta recalled,

> *"Nobody is really looking for robotics. They are all looking for how do we get fulfillment outcomes."*

This realization led to a crucial pivot in their thinking; they weren't a robotics company in supply chain, but a supply chain technology company using robotics as an enabler.

For their customers, success wasn't measured by how fast a bot moved or how sophisticated the technology was but by business metrics like reduced cost per unit, increased storage per square foot, and achieving 30-minute SLAs.

This focus on outcomes became their competitive edge. While competitors sold "robotic uptime," GreyOrange delivered fulfillment solutions. "We beat them all day long," Akash noted, "because, at the end of the day, that's what the customer is looking for." This mindset shapes everything—from resource allocation to product roadmap; every decision starts with customer outcomes, not technological improvements.

Fortune 100 customers reinforced this philosophy. These sophisticated customers conduct deep due diligence that cuts through marketing to focus on fundamental value. As Akash explained, "What they really are looking for is, 'Is the product good? Is the product real? Is the team good?" These customers think in five-year timeframes, focusing on long-term value rather than quick fixes or flashy features.

This focus on fundamental value rather than flashy features has become GreyOrange's north star. While competitors get caught up in speeds and specs, they stay focused on what customers actually care about—making their warehouses more efficient and profitable. It's a mindset that shapes not just their product roadmap but the entire company's DNA.

Made in India, built for the world

From a clunky robot assembled in a basement to sophisticated machines orchestrating Walmart's warehouses and from martial arts inspiration to health rings, the journeys of GreyOrange and Ultrahuman represent more than just startup success stories. They exemplify the newfound aspirations of Indian hardware founders.

Mohit's tweet captures this transformation perfectly.

Mohit Kumar
@deeppurpled

Excited to announce Ultrahuman's arrival in Japan
Great to partner with Softbank, Rakuten, Yahoo, Bic Camera, Yodobashi and Sourcenext.

We've done something that seemed almost impossible and funny a few quarters ago - 'A company from India selling devices in the Japanese market'

More on this coming soon :)

Ultrahuman @UltrahumanHQ · Oct 24, 2024
Konnichiwa Japan!

2:29 PM · Oct 24, 2024 · **45.5K** Views

The numbers tell part of the story: GreyOrange's leap to $100 million in revenue and Ultrahuman's growth from 20 rings daily to thousands monthly. But the bigger story is about what's possible. These companies have proven that with the right mindset—owning core manufacturing, thinking global from day one, building category-defying teams, moving fast while maintaining quality, and focusing on customer outcomes—hardware innovation can flourish anywhere.

Through their journeys, Akash and Mohit have not just crossed borders; they've erased them.

Building a Global Robotics Giant: Blume Ventures' Sanjay Nath on GreyOrange's Journey

Building a hardware company is notoriously challenging; building a global one from India seemed nearly impossible in 2011. Yet GreyOrange defied these odds to become a leader in warehouse automation. Sanjay Nath, Co-founder and Managing Partner at Blume Ventures and the company's first institutional investor, shares unique insights into the founders' journey, culture, and the milestones that shaped their success.

Q. What impressed you about the founding team in the early days? Any interesting anecdotes?

Akash and Samay were the pioneers of the robotics lab and were very involved in the CEL (Center for Entrepreneurship Learning) at BITS Pilani. Many don't know this, but they developed India's first humanoid robot, AcYut.

At BITS Pilani, they turned non-mandatory attendance into an opportunity, and went all in into building GreyOrange. The name 'GreyOrange' has a significant meaning; orange represents youth and energy for the future, while grey represents wisdom and past learnings.

They participated in an international robotics competition in Japan and came second to Honda! This got them international acclaim. I remember sitting with them in one of their first office. It was very simple and modest. One of them seemed distracted during our fundraising discussion, and when I asked what was on his mind, he said, 'I'm thinking of taking apart this electronic waste bin.' That's who they are. They're tinkerers, hands-on hardware engineers.

Q. Building a hardware company is hard. Why has the team been so successful internationally?

The integration of hardware and software as a platform is very interesting. They were pioneers of robotics-as-a-service. Very early on, they realized that GreyOrange needed to have its own factory. If you're going to automate customer shop flows and build a leading warehouse automation platform, you want to live, breathe, and eat that. You can't sit in an ivory tower and just code.

They hired well, understanding both product and distribution. They understood the sales side of scaling hardware.

Their international sequencing was also important. They understood that while China was yet up-and-coming, it was better to crack India first, then Southeast Asia (Hong Kong, Singapore), and then go to the US. Kerry Logistics, an early customer, adopted them in Singapore. Getting that international recognition in Southeast Asia and the Far East helped them become instrumental in transforming those initial warehouse successes into the US.

How would you describe the culture in the early days, and how has it evolved?

"'Work hard, play hard'—they knew that to become the best warehousing automation player in the world, the product had to iterate constantly. They held 24-hour hackathons twice a year and gave prizes to the best hardware engineers of the month. They had a very strong engineering and product culture, like Google, but with a hardware element, like Tesla.

They were focused on 'only settle for the best.' Their interviews were extremely rigorous. They would interview about a thousand to hire one. Initially, about 90% of their first 10-20 hires were from their college (BITS). While this helped in hitting the ground running, they later recognized the need for diversity in thinking and backgrounds.

Today, they've evolved into a global multi-product company. Akash has moved to Palo Alto along with their CFO. The headquarters are in the US, while India remains the nerve center and engine. They've brought in people with deep industry experience. Their challenge and opportunity is maintaining the balance between being institutional with seasoned industry professionals while retaining the original culture.

Q. Is there a milestone that made you especially proud?

Two significant funding milestones stand out. First was Tiger Global's investment—They sent an MIT robotics research scientist for two weeks of due diligence. The second was Mithril Capital's investment, getting Peter Thiel to invest was a real milestone.

But more than funding, what's really fantastic is seeing international leaders like H&M and Zara successfully deploying GreyOrange in their warehouses in Los Angeles, New York, and Europe. It makes you proud that those two boys we backed have evolved into an international brand. Today, with their new gStore product (The gStore SaaS software provides inventory management solutions to retail stores), they've moved from backend to frontend, becoming a full-stack platform. It's incredibly proud to know that if you bought something from H&M or Zara, GreyOrange has played such a critical role in streamlining and reducing the cost of that product to you.

Making Health More Trackable Than Ever Before: Blume's Karthik Reddy on Ultrahuman's Audacious Global Mission

The leap from running a food delivery business to building a global health tech platform isn't obvious. But for Ultrahuman founders Mohit Kumar and Vatsal Singhal, this transition was fueled by a deeper passion for health and fitness.

Karthik Reddy, Co-founder and Managing Partner at Blume Ventures, witnessed this evolution first-hand—From backing their previous venture Runnr to supporting their ambitious vision for Ultrahuman. In this candid conversation, he discusses why sometimes the best investments stem from founders' audacious dreams rather than perfect product-market fit, and how Ultrahuman is working to turn complex biomarker data into actionable health insights.

Q. Why did you decide to invest in Ultrahuman? What qualities of the founders and the company stood out to you the most?

Mohit and Vatsal were a part of the Runnr (acquired by Zomato) journey with Blume Fund II. They not only managed to reward the Fund with the fastest exit, an acquisition to Zomato but also continued to thrive and build the delivery business for Zomato, helping them compete effectively with Swiggy.

These journeys emboldened and prepared them for the passionate journey that was to unfold. Mohit had kept us abreast of his passion for health and fitness at a personal level and how he hoped to build something meaningful and global. When the relationship and the alignment for targeting problems on a large global market come together, it's a relatively easy decision to back such founders where history too is established. With a much smaller Fund III (as opposed to Fund IV), we played a smaller part of the first round but liked the direction enough that within a year, we played super pro rata and almost twice the initial check in the Series A round.

The problem area is what's known. The initial product iterations, much like consumer digital product ideas, were changed to usher in a long-term commitment, even if smaller audiences were interested in tracking biomarkers for the long term. We funded an app; we got to a wearables + biomarker company. That's the nature of early-stage investing.

Q. In 2020 wearables and biomarkers were quite new in the domestic market. What led to your conviction that the market would be ready for this? Has the shift in habit happened as quickly as you expected it to be?

Sometimes, it's the sheer audacity of entrepreneurs - it's not about products and specifics in such an early phase of the opportunity. In the pandemic, the current CBO, Bhuvan was moving from KKR to Ultrahuman. As an ex-med devices and healthcare expert, I could see his passion for the opportunity and I was also impressed that Mohit had managed to convince him of the vision that early in the journey. A deep knowledge and a desire to build a world-class health play kept coming through. VC is the design of such risk-taking.

Q. What do you think is the company's right to win? The wearable/health-tracking space is heating up, and many new companies are launching ring products.

The company's right to win is to be able to assemble talent from a decade of wearable learnings in the market and juxtapose it with the latest science in monitoring and measuring biomarkers. They have to be the best-integrated player globally and have the boldness to step where no one company has done before—we have watches, rings, high-end blood tests, various screening techniques, everything emerging—staying ahead of all of them in making simplicity come alive from the complexity of the human body is our right to win. Most data is dumb until someone makes it intelligent and customized - that's the mission here.

Section 2
Operators and Policy-Makers

Chapter 6
Soaring High

Aditya Ghosh's Guide to Building People-Centric Companies

1,40,000.

That's how many people Aditya Ghosh has interviewed personally during his 10-year tenure as President of IndiGo Airlines.

"I'm your biggest union leader," he would tell his pilots and flight attendants, and he really meant every word. He emphasized that employee satisfaction directly impacts customer experience in the airline business, and no employee concerns were too small for his attention. Missing water bottles in hotel rooms? Delayed cabs? Damaged luggage wheels? His door was always open.

The ROI of this high-touch approach?

It created a legacy that outlived his tenure at IndiGo. The numbers tell the story: Today, IndiGo commands more than 60% of the domestic market, has doubled revenue in the last five years, and ranks as the world's third-largest airline by market capitalization (as of December 2024). The foundation Aditya built continues to soar.

Years after moving on, Aditya continues to experience its ripple effects. During a recent flight, the co-pilot stepped out to greet him, and you guessed it right, he was an ex-IndiGo employee. A flight passenger from IndiGo's finance team, whom Aditya interviewed nine and a half years ago, recognized him. Even as he was deplaning, a captain with a baby in his arms stopped to remind him of the connection through his wife, a former IndiGo employee.

This story illustrates Aditya's core leadership principles: authentic connections with people aren't just good for morale; they're good for business.

Today, as cofounder of Akasa Air, Aditya is testing whether this high-touch leadership philosophy can scale beyond one success story to build India's next aviation giant. Here are his top lessons on building a legacy-leaving career.

Lesson 1 - Small tasks done diligently build big careers

Long before he became an aviation industry titan, Aditya Ghosh made a series of unconventional choices that would shape his life differently. In the mid-1990s, when India's brightest minds were racing toward engineering and medical schools, he chose a different path.

"I was pretty disillusioned with science in class 11 and 12," he recalled. Breaking from the herd mentality, Aditya enrolled in Delhi University to study history—a decision that raised eyebrows but taught him his first lesson about following his instincts.

After graduation, with a retired father and a younger brother still in school, the pressure to secure a job mounted. In newly liberalized India, his peers flocked to MBA programs.

Again, Aditya zigged where others zagged. "If I don't go to IIM Ahmedabad and graduate top of the class, I'm not getting a job at, say, BCG or McKinsey or Bain," he reasoned.

So he chose law, which was considered an "easy" course that "anybody could get into" at the time. The decision was so casual that he famously opened the entrance exam guide just days before the test. Yet this seemingly haphazard preparation landed him at J. Sagar Associates (JSA), one of India's premier law firms. As a Rs. 900-per-month intern at KNS Partners (JSA's IP-focused sister firm), Aditya discovered his defining philosophy: excellence isn't about perfect beginnings—it's about maximizing every opportunity through absolute dedication.

> *"If somebody gives you a job of photocopying papers, do it with diligence. Someone somewhere may notice you, no guarantees. And something better will happen, which will be far above and beyond your wildest expectation," he advised.*

His dedication soon landed him the role of Jyoti Sagar's executive assistant at just 21. "Working beside Jyoti gave me a front-row seat to India's economic transformation—from Bharti-Singtel to power sector privatization to FDI," he shared.

His diligence also impressed Rahul Bhatia, CEO of InterGlobe, a growing client at JSA. "Rahul Bhatia was very early on in bringing in professionals," Aditya recalled. "Since there was no in-house legal department at InterGlobe, all of the work was being done by me. Credit to Rahul that I was deeply involved in many of the business discussions."

This deep involvement would prove pivotal. After five years of handling InterGlobe's legal matters, Aditya had earned enough trust to land a seat at the historic meeting at Mumbai's Oberoi Hotel, where IndiGo Airlines was first conceptualized on a napkin.

Yet success brought its challenges. Seven years into a meteoric rise at JSA, Aditya wrestled with imposter syndrome. "I began questioning myself: am I really good? Or am I good because I started off as a little kid in JSA, and the partners just happened to like me?" The doubt gnawed at him, but his loyalty to JSA prevented him from joining another law firm. Instead, he secretly interviewed at GE for an in-house counsel position.

When Rahul Bhatia learned about this, his response revealed the instincts that would later build India's largest airline. Without hesitation, he pulled out a Post-it note. "Okay, then come and join us," he said, asking Aditya to write down his desired compensation. Within weeks, Aditya found himself working on what would become a pivotal document: the airline license application for IndiGo.

Aditya reflected, "I always say that opportunity knocks several times at everybody's door and I'm not saying it has to be out of greed or ambition, but just out of honesty or purpose, I think, one needs to actually try to take each one of those opportunities."

This philosophy of excellence in small tasks would later become the cornerstone of IndiGo's operational success. The same attention to detail that Aditya brought to photocopying papers would transform into the airline's renowned on-time performance and customer service standards.

From a Rs. 900-per-month intern to the architect of India's largest airline, Aditya's journey reveals a powerful truth: extraordinary careers aren't built on grand strategies alone but on the consistent pursuit of excellence in every task, no matter how small.

Lesson 2 - There's a business case for empathy

"Just an HR manager."

That's how a journalist criticized Aditya's tenure at IndiGo, contrasting him with 'true' CEOs. But what they meant as a criticism inadvertently highlighted what made him extraordinary. "For me, it's a badge of honor to feel that I am the Chief People Officer," Aditya responded, turning the intended slight into a manifesto for a different kind of leadership.

Aditya took an unconventional approach to leadership at IndiGo and now at Akasa: Every problem, no matter how trivial, deserves attention.

"When you're in an emergency room with a cut hand, you're in real pain," he explained. "The doctor might be treating a heart attack patient. But as the person with a cut hand, I'm expecting the same amount of attention from the doctor. As a CEO, your colleagues are expecting the same." This emergency room analogy captures the essence of his leadership philosophy: there are no small problems in a service business.

This insight became the cornerstone of his management philosophy. In an industry where CEOs typically focus on multi-billion-dollar aircraft deals and fuel hedging strategies, Aditya paid equal attention to delayed cabs and missing water bottles.

For Aditya, leadership begins with knowing your people beyond their employee IDs—a philosophy that led him to interview 140,000 people personally. While most CEOs would delegate hiring to HR, Aditya saw each interview as an investment in building trust. "You cannot disrespect somebody who you know," he explained. "Even if I have to scold you, I'll scold you like a parent, not as roll number 1378 on a list of 20,000 people."

In a world obsessed with metrics and bottom lines, Aditya's message is clear—if you're forced to define leadership in one word, it is empathy. Every person's problem, no matter how small it might seem in the grand scheme of things, deserves acknowledgment and respect.

> *"Think about the teachers you remember fondly," Aditya reflected. "It may not be the subject where you scored the highest. It could be a football teacher. It could be an English teacher. It could be a coach or whatever it is. It was somebody who did not give up on you. That's the leader that you keep going back to."*

Lesson 3 - Culture needs code

"It cannot happen by accident," Aditya emphasized when discussing how organizations achieve customer service excellence across thousands of touchpoints. He shared an anecdote to unpack this further. "A few months ago, I met one of the co-founders of Heads Up For Tails. I met him for the first time and said, 'I've never met you before, but I'm going to say you are doing something right. Any store I went to and any employee I talked to, they were all polite.' This is a great litmus test—on the front line when no one is watching, are your employees able to deliver high-quality service?"

It's not a coincidence—it's codified culture in action. Drawing from his experience scaling culture across organizations, Aditya has codified the process into four actionable pillars:

First, establish deep respect.

"All of us are equals here. We just have different roles to play," he emphasized. This is crucial in operations-heavy businesses where no single person, not even the CEO, can do everything. "You can't be the pilot, flight attendant, engineer, or security professional."

Second, practice instant recognition. "Recognition must be as immediate as criticism," Aditya insisted. He pointed out a common leadership flaw: while companies immediately react to mistakes, they rarely show the same urgency in recognizing good work.

> *"When something goes wrong, leaders react instantly. But when hundreds of things go right in the company, when somebody has*

stepped above and beyond, or somebody displayed a value that you hold dear, even in the face of hardship, we don't pick up the phone with the same amount of urgency," he remarked.

Third, behavior is contagious.

"When one person exhibits a behavior that's rewarded, more people start copying it and eventually everyone copies it. That's the power of culture. It's a set of acceptable behaviors."

Fourth, reward people meaningfully. Coming from low-margin businesses, Aditya learned that rewards can take many forms and don't always have to be monetary. He drew an interesting parallel with the military, "You win a battle, you do something well, you get promoted maybe once in five years. But every time you do something well, you're given an even more challenging operation to run. You're given an even more complex campaign to lead." That responsibility becomes the reward for the right person.

The true test of codified culture comes in critical moments. All you need to do is watch how employees handle difficult situations. "When there's a fog or a diversion, or there's a delayed flight, customers are screaming, and my colleagues would be standing there listening patiently." That kind of composure under pressure—it's the result of consistently reinforced cultural values.

The key insight? Building a high-performance organization isn't about grand gestures or hefty bonuses. When culture is properly coded into an organization's DNA, excellence becomes not just an aspiration but an operational standard.

Lesson 4 - Build structural advantages from day one

Why would someone who built India's largest airline return to the same brutally competitive industry? For Aditya, the answer lies in a lesson he learned building IndiGo: when you engineer structural advantages from day one, you create moats that competitors can't cross even decades later.

He points to a striking market inefficiency:

> *"India is a very large market with very low aircraft penetration. In 2005-2006, there was one passenger aircraft for every 50,000 Americans and one passenger aircraft for every 2.4 million Indians. Today, it is about 3 million Indians for one aircraft. We added 300 million people to our population since 2005 but added only 400 aircraft."*

This massive untapped potential represents a trillion-dollar opportunity—but only for those who can build superior cost architectures.

"The real success comes from having the sharpest cost structure," he emphasized. "Because the revenue side is commoditized. Today, if you open up an online travel portal and do a Delhi, Bombay ticket, all the airlines are likely a few rupees off each other."

Drawing from his experience building two airlines, Aditya breaks down the anatomy of costs: 40% fuel, 20% aircraft ownership and leases, 10-15% payroll, and the remainder in maintenance and other expenses. With most costs denominated in dollars but revenue in rupees, the margin for error in India is razor-thin.

The key, Aditya learned, is building structural cost advantages from day one that compound over time:

Start with fuel efficiency. While using newer aircraft with better fuel-burning technology might save only 1-5% compared to competitors, in a business of "billion-dollar ideas," these margins matter enormously.

Time your investments strategically. "It's no coincidence that IndiGo's first hundred aircraft order came after 9/11 or that Akasa's initial 76-plane order (later expanded to 226) followed the pandemic." he explained.

Plan comprehensively, Aditya emphasized. "You ordered the airplanes, but you haven't ordered the engines. You've ordered the engines, but you haven't done the long-term maintenance contract. You cannot create predictability of cost." Every component needs strategic consideration.

These structural advantages, once secured, become nearly impossible for competitors to overcome. "That cost advantage is set in stone. You cannot change that anymore."

While Aditya's examples come from aviation, his framework for building structural advantages applies universally. As India adds hundreds of millions of consumers to the middle class, the winners won't just be those who understand the market—they'll be the ones who build cost advantages that allow them to serve it profitably at scale.

Lesson 5 - Great businesses are built on complementary partnerships

When asked about the secret sauce behind IndiGo's success, Aditya Ghosh doesn't hesitate. "I do think it's a pretty unique combination," he said of the partnership between Rahul Bhatia and Rakesh Gangwal that created India's largest airline.

The beauty of their partnership lay not in their similarities but in their differences. "They both come with extremely complementary skills," Aditya explained, "but with a deep respect for what the other person is bringing to the table."

This wasn't just about dividing responsibilities. It was about how two different worldviews could create something greater than the sum of their parts. Rahul Bhatia, through InterGlobe, had built a successful travel services business in India and had the vision to bet on India's potential two decades before it became fashionable. Rakesh Gangwal, whom Aditya describes as "the smartest airline brain in the world," brought deep aviation expertise from his time as one of the highest-ranking Indians in the US aviation industry.

But what made this partnership truly special was their shared values and approach to business.

> *"While both of them are very understated people, very down to earth, they're not chasing private jets and sailboats," Aditya noted, "they both have tremendous zeal to pursue excellence relentlessly."*

Their different yet complementary approaches to management created a perfect balance. Aditya recalled his annual meetings with Rakesh, "It was extremely painful because he was relentless, and he would say five things at the end of those five days where I'd be like, 'how did I not think of this looking into this business every day?'" But then, characteristic of his understated style, "that meeting would finish and the next thing was, 'okay, are we going to dinner at Haldiram or going to have an ice cream?'"

Meanwhile, Rahul Bhatia's genius lies in his ability to delegate and trust his team. "If delegation was an art form, Rahul Bhatia is a Michelangelo," Aditya said. This trust was evident in how he handled Aditya's hiring—responding to news of Aditya interviewing elsewhere by simply handing him a Post-it note to write down his desired compensation.

The impact of this complementary partnership extended beyond business success. It created a culture where the management team had the freedom to execute while having access to world-class strategic insights. As Aditya put it, "They were like, 'We're investors, and let the management team do its thing.'"

The key takeaway? In building great businesses, sometimes the most powerful partnerships aren't between people who think alike but between those who think differently yet respect each other's strengths. It's about finding partners whose skills complement yours, whose values align with yours, and who can challenge you to see things you might miss while looking at the business daily.

What makes Aditya Ghosh special?

Growing up in a New Delhi government employee housing

colony in the 1980s and 90s might seem unremarkable, but for Aditya, it laid the foundation for his leadership philosophy. These early years taught him invaluable lessons about equality, humility, and the true measures of success.

"Everybody wears the same kind of clothes. Everybody goes to the same kind of school," he recalled. In this world, where a tennis racket was a once-in-few-years luxury and new clothes were an annual event, success was measured differently. Parents, many of whom held significant positions in India's liberalization story, never discussed titles or achievements—they emphasized character and capabilities.

The environment shaped his view of excellence. Surrounded by neighbors who balanced IIT studies with cricket, music, and other pursuits, Aditya learned that true achievement transcends conventional metrics. "Your badge of honor wasn't your mark sheet," he emphasizes. "It was your ability to excel across dimensions."

This foundation of empathy continues to shape his leadership today. A recent social media exchange perfectly captures its essence. When a user caustically criticized Aditya for "not being a true entrepreneur" and "just piggybacking on Vinay Dubey at Akasa and Anjan Chatterjee at Chourangi," Aditya's response was characteristic of his leadership philosophy.

"I don't know whether I'm an entrepreneur or not. Have I started something completely by myself? I don't think I have." he acknowledged without hesitation. "Even at Chourangi, where I'm an equal owner with Anjan, I ride on his coat tail.." This ability to acknowledge and learn from others' strengths, rather than claiming sole credit, exemplifies his leadership style.

In an era obsessed with founder-CEOs and unicorn valuations, Aditya offers a different leadership model. His success—from scaling India's largest airline to building new ventures—comes not from claiming the spotlight but from shining it on others.

The lessons from that government colony continue to resonate: true impact comes not from titles or valuations but from the ability to build lasting institutions through humility, continuous learning, and unwavering focus on people.

Chapter 7

The OG Bureaucrat Entrepreneur

How Amitabh Kant Engineered India's Transformation

A few decades ago, a crisis was brewing along Kerala's vibrant coastline. Despite their dawn-to-dusk struggles with the Arabian Sea, the state's fisher folk were caught in a sticky net–they were getting only a fraction of the market price for their catch. The rest of it went to the middlemen.

Enter Amitabh Kant, a 1980-batch IAS officer who had just taken the helm as Managing Director of Matsyafed, Kerala State's Co-operative Federation for Fisheries Development Ltd, after his stint as the Sub Collector of Thalassery (Kannur district).

Within days, Amitabh launched into action with the mindset of a founder solving a market inefficiency. He introduced beach-level auctions and invested in new technology, like fiberglass crafts and disco nets, so that they could go farther into the sea for a better catch. His team even opened bank accounts for them in an era when opening an account was often a painfully long, tedious process.

He didn't stop there and addressed the entire value chain. Amitabh's team formed self-help groups for fisher folk and launched exclusive buses where fisher-women could store their baskets in the back while sitting comfortably in the front.

This whole 'revolution' of sorts happened within a short span of four years.

Think of it as building a modern-era fish marketplace. It was 'entrepreneurship from within the government' at its best.

This early success story would become Amitabh Kant's signature approach: bringing entrepreneurial thinking to bureaucracy. Over the next four and a half decades, he would repeatedly demonstrate how government officials could act as catalysts for transformation in tourism, ease of doing business, or digital infrastructure.

Amitabh Kant is, arguably, India's OG bureaucrat entrepreneur.

Today, as India's startup ecosystem races toward global prominence, the need for such bureaucrat entrepreneurs has never been greater. Amitabh Kant's four-and-a-half-decade career gives us the blueprint for becoming one.

We've tried to uncover how he does what he does by diving deep into his many avatars across some of India's biggest public endeavors–initiatives that would go on to define India's policy-making landscape on the global stage.

Lesson 1 - Think local, scale global

After a ~3.5-year stint as the District Collector in Kozhikode, where he went head-on against the public space encroachments, Amitabh Kant found himself in a 'punishment posting' as the Secretary of Tourism for Kerala. At the time, Kerala was barely a blip on India's tourism radar.

"Nobody had heard of Kerala as a tourism destination at

that point," Amitabh recalled.

> *"Everyone went to Kashmir or Rajasthan, but nobody traveled to Kerala. I decided to use this punishment posting as an opportunity to transform Kerala tourism."*

Instead of accepting the status quo, Amitabh orchestrated a bold return to Kerala's cultural roots.

"I brought back traditional Kerala architecture, starting with the Nalukettu houses," he explained. The strategy was comprehensive-introducing backwater tourism, repositioning Ayurveda from mere massage to serious 21-day therapy, and reviving traditional art forms like Koodiyattam, Kathakali, and Mohiniyattam.

The revival extended beyond architecture and wellness. Amitabh promoted Kerala's martial art, Kalaripayattu, and its distinctive cuisine—elements that would become central to the state's tourism identity.

"We differentiated Kerala from the rest of the world by embracing what made us unique: our traditional arts, culture, martial arts, backwaters, and Ayurveda," Amitabh explained.

The strategy's success exceeded all expectations. In just three years, Kerala achieved what seemed impossible: National Geographic Traveler, the world's premier travel magazine, ranked this previously unknown destination among its ten exotic paradises.

"The National Geographic recognition was significant," Amitabh recalled. "Bill McKibben highlighted something unique—Kerala wasn't just beautiful, it was the only global destination with quality of life and human development indices that surpassed Western standards."

AN ARTICLE FROM NATIONAL GEOGRAPHIC TRAVELER SUBSCRIBENOW!

Kerala, India

By Bill McKibben

Contenders battle in a Snakeboat Race at the Onam Festival.

Photograph © Lindsay Hebberd/CORBIS

Kerala is a very easy place to simply sit back and enjoy. The name means "land of coconuts," and the palms shade nearly the entire state from the tropical sun; many call the beach at Kovalam the best in India; visitors can spend a day riding small ferries through the backwater lagoons or watching elephants cavort in the wildlife sanctuaries; the spicy food may be the best vegetarian cuisine on the planet.

But for me, the real reason to visit Kerala, which lies at the southwestern tip of the subcontinent, is for the *intellectual* adventure: Kerala is a bizarre anomaly among developing nations, a place that offers real hope for the future of the Third World. Consider: This small state in India, though not much larger than Maryland, has a population as big as California's and a per capita annual income of less than $300. But its infant mortality rate is low, its literacy rate among the highest on Earth, and its birthrate below America's and falling faster. Kerala's citizens live nearly as long as Americans or Europeans. Though mostly a land of paddy-covered plains, statistically Kerala stands out as the Mount Everest of social development; there's truly no place like it.

In the mornings, from nearly anywhere in Kerala, you can hear loud music from the Hindu temples, wailing muezzins at the mosques, and church bells ringing at the cathedrals. Religious tolerance is just one reason for Kerala's success. The state government has effected sweeping land reforms and spends almost half of its budget on health and education. A heritage of female-headed households means women have always been equal participants here. Unlike almost everywhere else in Asia, women outnumber men in Kerala, suggesting that there has been no selective abortion or female infanticide.

Kerala is not a quiet spot. It has a rate of newspaper readership that is among the highest in the world and plenty of never-ending political arguments. Parades of striking bus drivers or medical students or *kathakali* dancers block traffic in the capital of Trivandrum almost daily. But for me, that engagement with the world is one of the best things about the place. Keralites meet you on more or less equal terms, with neither the subservience nor the rage you'll find in much of the Third World.

Kerala is a place to meander: Simply take a bus from Trivandrum or Cochin out to almost any village and spend a day wandering the dikes between the rice paddies and rubber trees, seeing how half the world still lives: men and women stooping to cut rice with sickles, or spreading coconut along the road to dry; water buffalo wallowing in the irrigation ditches; every inch of ground cultivated; every small field lined with palms; a place where little is wasted. It's also a place that works, and in poor, rural Asia, that alone would make Kerala a paradise. The breeze rustling the palm fronds is just a bonus.

The information in this story was accurate at the time it was published, but we suggest you confirm all details before making travel plans.

Source: National Geographic Website

However, the most revolutionary aspect of this transformation was Amitabh's approach to implementation.

"I recognized early that government shouldn't be the driver—we needed to empower the private sector," he explained. "Government's role was to enable through land allocation, credit access, and brand building. The actual development and operations had to come from entrepreneurs."

This approach proved to be a masterstroke.

"Kerala's success wasn't built on five-star hotels. It was built on boutique resorts, local entrepreneurship, authentic art, culture, and cuisine."

"The multiplier impact on jobs was enormous. For every direct job created, there were 12, 13 indirect jobs being created, and jobs were being created for women."

Kerala truly became 'God's Own Country.'

However, Amitabh wasn't done with tourism yet, or rather, tourism wasn't done with him.

"I wanted to go to the finance ministry," Amitabh recalled when he applied for a central government posting after all his 'God's Own Country' project.

The Civil Services Board approved his selection, but fate had other plans. A call from Brajesh Mishra, the Principal Secretary to the then-Prime Minister Atal Bihari Vajpayee, would change his trajectory.

The conversation was brief but defining. "Have you applied for Delhi?" asked the Principal Secretary. When Amitabh confirmed, Mishra reminded him of their earlier conversation when the PM came to Kerala, and he was responsible for the arrangements.

"So, Brajesh Mishra said, 'You remember our conversation.

We'll post you to tourism.' When I mentioned there were no vacancies, he simply said they would create one. That's how I found myself at the tourism ministry."

Amitabh's arrival at the tourism ministry coincided with a perfect storm of crises.

"The minute I landed, within a month and a half of that, the twin tower blast happened. And then there was a war in Afghanistan. There was an attack on our Parliament, and there were several travel advisories against travel to the South Asian regions, particularly India. Our already limited hotel industry saw occupancy plummet to 10-15%."

This crisis catalyzed one of India's most innovative marketing initiatives. While other Asian nations pulled back their tourism campaigns, Amitabh saw an opportunity. "We went straight to the consumer and we launched the Incredible India campaign. Indonesia, Malaysia, Thailand, all had withdrawn their campaigns. We launched it at the peak of that crisis and we brought tourism back to India," Amitabh remembered.

The campaign marked a pivotal shift in how the world perceived India. The stark visuals and bold storytelling challenged stereotypes, presenting India not as a land of snake charmers but as a complex tapestry of experiences—from luxury to adventure, wellness to spirituality. International media took notice. Travel writers who had relegated India to backpacker stories featured it in luxury columns. Even skeptical tour operators who had written off South Asia began reconsidering their stance.

The transformation was reflected in the numbers. "This led to our hotels getting 100% occupancy. Demand just blossomed and that led to new airports being created in Hyderabad, Bengaluru, Mumbai, Delhi, because it was a marketing-led strategy to drive growth."

From transforming Kerala into 'God's Own Country' to re-branding an entire nation as 'Incredible India,' Amitabh demonstrated the power of entrepreneurial thinking in governance. But for him, these tourism triumphs weren't just successes—they were proof of concept. This wouldn't be the last time Amitabh would deploy this playbook—it was just the beginning.

Lesson 2 - Build ecosystems, don't just stop at policies

When Prime Minister Narendra Modi took office in 2014, India's business landscape was choked by bureaucratic hurdles. Despite its economic potential, India was ranked 142nd in the World Bank's ease of doing business index. It was a stark reminder of how far the world's fastest-growing major economy had to go. For Amitabh Kant, the newly appointed Secretary of Industrial Policy and Promotion, this was a call to action.

"The Prime Minister said, go after the ease of doing business," Amitabh remembered. "We were full of procedures, rules, regulations at that time. Everything was done through long paper forms. Nothing was digital."

What followed was the most ambitious regulatory transformation attempt in India's history. Amitabh orchestrated a complex choreography involving over 40 ministries and state governments, each with entrenched processes and resistance to change.

India leaped 79 positions in just three years. However, PM Modi's and Amitabh Kant's masterstroke was introducing competition among states.

Amitabh explained, "The first year we did this, Gujarat came number one. Next year, Andhra beat Gujarat, and in the third year, Telangana beat Andhra and Gujarat. (It) was a lot of hard work with the ministries to change mindsets, to change forms, to change procedures, which is very tough in government. But a lot was achieved."

However, the most remarkable transformations came from unexpected quarters.

> *"The good thing was that Jharkhand and Chhattisgarh, which were 24th and 25th, have jumped to 4th and 5th position. The Prime Minister said, 'Make the states compete. If you make the states compete, they improve.'," said Amitabh.*

The reforms didn't stop there; in fact, they were just getting started.

Under Amitabh's leadership, India's Foreign Direct Investment (FDI) regime radically transformed. "Today, 98% of the FDI comes through the automatic route," he noted.

Then, in 2016, one of India's most ambitious initiatives, Startup India, was launched.

"When we launched Startup India, we had barely 200 registered startups," Amitabh recalled. "Today, that number stands at 140,000."

"Before we launched Startup India, we did a lot of groundwork," Amitabh recalled. "We removed the government rules, regulation procedures, away from startups. We brought in incubators and brought the whole ecosystem of Atal Innovation Mission. We even opened tinkering labs in schools. And it's been a huge success story. We've been able to build up the third-best ecosystem in a very short while."

Beyond regulatory reforms, Amitabh championed the revolutionary potential of India's digital public infrastructure (DPI).

For the uninitiated, India has a unique digital public infrastructure—an open-source, inter-operable platform that serves as a digital highway for innovation. This shared digital foundation has enabled startups to build services such as instant payments, quick loans, or lightning-fast insurance policies that can reach millions of Indians within minutes.

"India now processes 46% of the world's real-time digital payments," Amitabh noted. "China, in second place, accounts for only 18%."

This digital infrastructure has spawned a new generation of entrepreneurs. "The startups can provide insurance in 30 seconds now," Amitabh explained. "This has not happened anywhere else." What makes this transformation unique is its democratic nature. "The data belongs to the citizen," Amitabh emphasized.

The model has proved so successful that about 20 countries are now adopting India's DPI blueprint.

Lesson 3 - Master the art of high-stakes negotiation

In December 2022, as India assumed the G20 presidency amid significant global turbulence, Amitabh faced perhaps his most complex challenge yet. The task: forge consensus among deeply divided nations on a host of crucial issues. The Prime Minister's mandate was clear: make it action-oriented, ambitious, and inclusive. "This opportunity comes once in 20 years," Amitabh said. "And we had to do it to perfection."

The scale of the diplomatic puzzle was staggering. With the Russia-Ukraine conflict straining international relations and the Global South demanding a greater voice, traditional diplomatic playbooks seemed inadequate.

The first test of Amitabh's leadership came not in the negotiating rooms with global leaders but in building a team that could navigate this diplomatic labyrinth.

"I had to communicate the Prime Minister's vision to everyone and get everybody to act to that vision," said Amitabh.

"We did a lot of risk-taking, a lot of aggressive negotiations, a lot of brinkmanship," Amitabh noted. "But all that could be done because we were clear about the vision of achieving success for India."

Next came the seemingly impossible task of creating a document that maintains consensus while being ambitious and inclusive. The numbers alone tell a story of diplomatic persistence. "One paragraph on Russia, China took us 300 hours of negotiation, 16 drafts failed. We had to do about close to 250 bilaterals, but we were very clear that we'll achieve consensus at the end of it."

This clear thinking allowed India to amplify the Global South's priorities.

"Work on principles which will apply to everybody. Don't get into this business of naming and condemning others. We were very clear that we are going to be the voice of the global South. If tomorrow 60% of the growth is going to come from emerging markets in the global South, then speak that voice out and we did it very strongly."

Think Big, Think Global: A blueprint for India's $35 Trillion dream

History offers a clear lesson about economic transformation. "No country in the world, post World War II, has grown without penetrating global markets," said Amitabh. Whether it was Japan, Korea, Taiwan, Singapore, or, more recently, China, the pattern is clear. For Amitabh, the implications for Indian startups are obvious–thinking local isn't enough.

> *"The market for Indian startups is not just the 1.4 billion people of India," Amitabh emphasizes. "It's the 5 to 6 billion people who will be moving from poverty to middle class in the next 5 to 6 years."*

This isn't just aspiration—it's existential. Every period of India's highest growth, he pointed out, has coincided with export booms.

However, the opportunity landscape is shifting rapidly. "Whether it's electric vehicles, battery storage, quantum computing, or green hydrogen," Amitabh explained, "these are the emerging battlegrounds of global innovation." For India's entrepreneurs, these represent not just opportunities but imperatives.

This global ambition comes at a pivotal moment in India's journey.

"If you want to be a Viksit Bharat," Amitabh emphasized, "we are talking about taking your GDP close to $30-35 trillion by 2047." The implications are staggering—per capita income must leap from $2,500 to at least $14,000. "That would mean a quantum jump in not merely the services sector, which is important, but you need to be transformational in manufacturing. You need to raise your agriculture productivity. You need to do cutting-edge work on new urbanization."

Amitabh argued that this transformation needs to be holistic. "We need 10,000 large companies," he explains. The large companies then create the ecosystem for MSMEs and tier II, III, and IV producers." But the revolution must extend beyond business. "India needs to improve its learning outcomes, health outcomes, and nutritional standards. The rising human development index is very critical."

But who will drive this transformation, along with founders and operators?

Bureaucrats who think like them, of course!

"Actually, I really believe that a lot more officers should be intra-entrepreneurial within government," Amitabh noted. "They should start their career as startup officers within the government."

Based on his decades of experience, Amitabh has identified

three essential qualities that set exceptional bureaucrats apart. "One is a huge amount of positivity and optimism. The will to change and people who are not status quo-ist, who want to transform the system. And thirdly, I look for people who think big in terms of the next 15 years."

Amitabh's journey offers a blueprint for bureaucratic entrepreneurship: think big but start specific, build coalitions across stakeholders, and always keep sight of the end user—whether a Kerala fisher-woman or a first-time entrepreneur.

As India charts its course toward 2047, this blueprint for bureaucratic entrepreneurship couldn't be more timely. The next generation of civil servants would do well to remember: transformation doesn't just happen—it must be engineered, one bold initiative at a time.

Chapter 8
Built to Endure

The Tata Manual for Timeless Institution Building

In late 1994, fresh from Oxford University, Rhodes Scholar Mukund Rajan sat before the Tata Administrative Services (TAS) panel. For India's most ambitious graduates, TAS—the elite leadership program of the country's most respected business house—represented what the Indian Administrative Service meant for public service: a path to the highest echelons of leadership.

Little did he know that this interview would mark the beginning of a transformative 23-year journey with one of India's, nay, cancel that, the world's most respected business houses.

The interview was particularly special because Ratan Tata himself was present. Like President Kennedy, who famously surrounded himself with Rhodes Scholars, Ratan Tata had an eye for exceptional talent and saw something special in the young candidate.

As Dr. Mukund Rajan recalled, "Somebody in the Tata Administrative Service Secretariat told me that he had said, 'I need to get this guy in my office once he finishes the obligatory first year of training.'"

This moment exemplifies the Tata Group's distinctive approach to talent: looking beyond conventional metrics to identify individuals capable of stewarding not just a business, but a legacy.

The story that unfolds through Mukund's journey from being Ratan Tata's executive assistant to becoming the group's first Brand Custodian offers invaluable lessons for modern business leaders and entrepreneurs.

Through his unique vantage point of working closely with Ratan Tata and witnessing the group's transformation into a global powerhouse, Mukund's experiences illuminate five crucial lessons relevant for any organization aspiring to build a global legacy while staying true to its Indian roots. The first of these lessons emerges from a decision that would define the Group's approach to value creation.

Lesson 1 - Patient capital delivers extraordinary dividends

In the late 1990s, at the height of the dot-com bubble, the Tata Group faced a decision that would test its foundational principles and define its approach to value creation for decades to come.

The markets were frothy, tech stocks were soaring, and TCS, the Group's crown jewel in information technology, held the key to an unprecedented corporate restructuring. A simple back-of-the-envelope calculation revealed that listing TCS at that point and diluting a small percentage of equity could raise enough capital for Tatas to take every single one of their listed companies private.

Every single one.

For a conglomerate whose ownership had been progressively diluted—to the point where the Birlas once held a larger stake in Tata Steel than the Tatas themselves—this represented a rare opportunity to re-consolidate control.

However, what happened next would become a defining example of the Tata way of doing business. Dr. Mukund Rajan recalled, "When push came to shove, and Mr Tata was presented with the data, he took the view that we would not list TCS at that point in time."

The reason?

"He felt the markets are very frothy, and we are going to be here another hundred years. We can't afford to play this quarter-on-quarter kind of game."

This decision, made at the peak of market exuberance, exemplified the distinction between being an opportunistic businessman vs. institutional stewardship. It wasn't the only time the Group would choose long-term value over short-term gains. The same philosophy of patient capital would be tested again in the Group's persistent pursuit of its aviation ambitions.

The group faced repeated setbacks, from the nationalization of Air India under JRD Tata to the regulatory hurdles of the 1990s. Yet, they never compromised their principles. When blocked from partnering with Singapore Airlines, Ratan Tata took the unprecedented step of sending a handwritten letter to the then Prime Minister Late Mr. Atal Bihari

Vajpayee. Mukund describes this letter as "probably the fiercest condemnation of government policy that you would see from a corporate leader to the head of Government in India, in any regime."

This steadfast adherence to principles yielded dividends decades later. When the aviation policy finally changed in 2013, Singapore Airlines, which "could have gone to anybody in India, to the Ambanis, to Adani, to Birlas," chose to return to the Tatas. Mukund observed, "That tells you a story that culture, values, the esteem in which a group is held can really pay long-term dividends."

The ultimate test of this long-term orientation came when business imperatives clashed with social commitments in West Bengal.

When the controversial Nano plant relocation from Singur made headlines, many expected the Tatas to withdraw all their investments from the state. However, Ratan Tata made a clear distinction between political challenges and social commitment. True to its commitment, it continued building the Tata Medical Centre in Kolkata.

The hospital, promised alongside the Singur plant investment, was inaugurated in 2011 as a world-class cancer treatment facility. Drawing on the expertise of Mumbai's Tata Memorial Hospital, it served a critical need in a state that previously had no access to specialized cancer treatment.

Mukund noted in his book 'The Brand Custodian: My Years with the Tatas,' "The Tata commitment was delivered in full, never mind that the state government had failed to deliver."

In each of these three episodes—the TCS listing restraint, the aviation sector persistence, and the West Bengal commitment— the Group chose the harder but more enduring path. These instances demonstrate how principled leadership, focused beyond short-term gains, builds institutions that endure for centuries.

Lesson 2 - Question the unquestioned. Always!

In the 1980s, as India's protected economy lulled most businesses into complacency, Ratan Tata was charting a radically different course for Tata Industries. While his contemporaries focused on defending their domestic turf, he was already mapping the Group's entry into process control industries and positioning for the IT revolution sweeping through the United States.

The Tata spirit of challenging the status quo wasn't new. Mukund noted, "The founder of the Tata group, Jamshedji Tata, was extremely well-traveled. He made his early fortune in China, working out of Shanghai at a time when very few Indians ventured to those parts of the world." This pioneering spirit, woven into the Group's DNA by its founder, would find its most dramatic expression under Ratan Tata's leadership.

His forward-thinking mindset would prove crucial when India's economic liberalization arrived in the 1990s. While the influential 'Bombay Club' of industrialists lobbied for continued protectionism, Ratan Tata emerged as a powerful contrarian voice.

"He was famously one of the people who said, 'no, because

if we continue this protection, we will never catch up. We've already lost decades'," recalled Mukund. This stance wasn't just about policy—it represented fundamentally questioning the defensive mindset that had dominated Indian business thinking.

Mukund's experience with the Tata Opportunities Fund offers the most striking example of the 'Question the Unquestioned' philosophy in action. He was asked to be the fund's founding Managing Partner despite never having done private equity before.

When they started marketing the fund, they were told they had "zero chance of success" because of an inherent conflict of interest: it was a Tata-sponsored fund investing in Tata companies. Critics said "nobody in their right mind" would invest in such a structure.

However, the team didn't back down. Instead, they achieved "probably the fastest first close at 400 million for an Indian fund in 4 months." Reflecting on this success, he echoed Ratan Tata's philosophy:

> ***"Never accept somebody's negativity. Never accept that something can't be done until you've actually given it a damn good shot."***

This spirit of challenging conventions while staying true to core values is the hallmark of Ratan Tata's legacy. From developing one of India's first indigenously designed and developed passenger cars, the Tata Indica, to backing ambitious startups in his later years, he consistently proved that transformative innovation emerges not just from questioning conventions but from having the courage to act on those questions. In each case, the Group's success came not from following the path well-traveled but from daring to ask: "What if?"

Lesson 3 - Engineer purpose into profit

At the heart of the Tata Group lies a radical innovation in corporate structure. "The ownership structure is quite unique. In fact, there are probably no exact parallels anywhere in the world," explained Dr. Mukund Rajan, describing what makes the Tata Group unique.

At its core lies an extraordinary arrangement: a holding company largely owned by not-for-profit trusts, creating a mechanism where corporate success automatically translates into societal good. Every rupee of profit, every business milestone achieved, flows back to fuel charitable initiatives. It's capitalism engineered to serve society.

This isn't just a noble idea on paper. Its influence permeates every level of the organization. "For employees in the Group, there is a sense that you're serving a larger purpose: the harder you work, the more good work gets done in society," Mukund explained. The Tata Trusts, among India's largest charities, has funded almost every significant non-profit initiative in the country's history.

The Group's mission statement crystallizes this philosophy, "to improve the quality of life of the communities we serve."

What's striking about this mission isn't what it says but what it omits: there's no mention of market leadership, shareholder returns, or profit maximization. The focus is singularly on community impact. This alignment between ownership structure and mission creates what Mukund calls "a group with a difference."

> ***"I think people, stakeholders, and the average retail customer see this and then see, 'Okay, this is a group with a difference.' This is somebody that I can trust. And that then becomes your biggest card in the market."***

This wasn't just corporate virtue signaling. In an era of corporate excess, Ratan Tata was known for his understated presence. He carried his own bags at airports, avoided large security entourages, and maintained a simple lifestyle.

This wasn't just personal preference; it was leadership by example. Mukund observed, "Today, you see people who would like to flaunt the entourage around them, the security personnel with 10 guns. He had none of that. He didn't want that." In Tata's world, modesty wasn't just a virtue; it was a statement of values.

The Tata model offers a profound insight for modern entrepreneurs: while their unique ownership structure may be impossible to replicate, its underlying principle—that profit serves a purpose rather than defining it—is universal. In an age where stakeholder capitalism has become a buzzword, the Tata Group stands as living proof that embedding social purpose into corporate DNA isn't just ethically sound; it's a superior way of doing business.

Lesson 4 - Keep up with the times

When Ratan Tata took the helm, he confronted a unique challenge: fragmentation. The Group's disparate businesses "often quite looked different from each other in terms of their visual identity and branding," as Mukund observed in his book.

This fragmentation wasn't just cosmetic; it reflected deeper barriers to creating a unified culture across a diverse conglomerate. The Group's response to this challenge would become a masterclass in evolving while maintaining core values.

The first step was visual cohesion. Ratan Tata engaged Wolff Olins, the renowned corporate identity specialist, to craft a new Group Composite Mark. Working with Wally Olins, the team created more than just a logo; they built a unified identity system.

Companies without 'Tata' in their name, from Rallis to Voltas, were linked to the mother brand through the designation "A Tata Enterprise." This visual evolution created what the team called "a sense of shared identity and even shared destiny within the group."

While visual cohesion was crucial, the true test of cultural evolution arrived with the Group's international expansion—a challenge that would demand more than just unified branding.

The Tetley acquisition in 2000, at $450 million, was the largest in Indian corporate history at that time and became a template for cultural integration.

The Tatas established clear ground rules: no wholesale firing of senior leaders, minimal lateral induction of Indian managers, and deep respect for local heritage, down to beloved brand elements like the Tetley 'folk' cartoon characters.

This wasn't just about preserving what worked; it was about Tatas permeating their work ethic into an international business through cultural osmosis. Two decades later, Tetley remains one of Britain's most beloved tea brands, proving that respecting local heritage while introducing Tata values creates lasting success.

The most nuanced expression of this cultural evolution was the transformation of the Group's Code of Conduct, a document that needed to bridge not just geographies but also generations and value systems.

In 1998, when the Code was first written, it read like "Moses and the Ten Commandments," as Mukund humorously recalled. The document was a product of its time—male-centric with no mention of "she," focused solely on India's development, and written in a commanding, top-down tone.

But as the Tata Group expanded globally and society evolved, so did the need to re-imagine this crucial document. The journey of transformation happened in three distinct waves.

First came the geographical evolution. With acquisitions like Corus and Jaguar Land Rover, the Code shifted from solely developing the Indian economy to supporting the economies wherever Tatas operated. A British employee at JLR would now be committed to Britain's growth, just as an Indian employee would be to India's.

Then came the societal evolution. The Code became gender-neutral, reflecting changing workplace demographics and values. But, perhaps most telling was the cultural nuance required for the whistle-blower clause. What seemed straightforward in India needed careful rewording in France and Germany, where historical experiences with the Nazis and Stasi had made the very concept of "whistle-blowing" problematic. Mukund explained, "We had to reword it so it didn't sound like we were asking people to rat on their colleagues."

Finally, in 2015 came the generational evolution. Recognizing a younger workforce, the Code's tone shifted from prescriptive to conversational. Instead of "thou shalt not," it offered practical illustrations of ethical dilemmas and their resolutions. It became a living document that guided rather than commanded.

Yet throughout these transformations, as Mukund emphasized, "At the heart of it, the basic values all remain the same."

The evolution of the Code exemplifies a broader truth about institutional building: successful cultural transformation isn't about abandoning principles but finding contemporary expressions for timeless values. In the Tata experience, evolution became not just a response to change but a source of competitive advantage.

Lesson 5 - Bet on young leaders

When Dr. Mukund Rajan joined Tatas, he lacked what was considered the golden ticket to success in corporate India: an MBA.

Yet, within years, he found himself sitting on the boards of major telecom companies, becoming their youngest director. Before 40, he was CEO of one of the Group's largest listed companies, Tata Teleservices (Maharastra) Limited. This wasn't an accident but a manifestation of Ratan Tata's distinctive philosophy about talent and leadership.

"What I would credit him with," Mukund explained, "goes back to his early years on the Tata Sons board." As its youngest director, Ratan Tata had experienced firsthand how colleagues "2-3 decades older" could have very different willingness to take risk. These formative experiences shaped his unconventional approach to nurturing young talent.

"He had no preconceived notions," Mukund noted. "For him, your age or experience didn't matter. He was more interested in what kind of imagination you showed, what ideas you had, and your ability to lead people."

This commitment to youth wasn't mere tokenism—it was about entrusting consequential decisions to emerging leaders. The development of the Indica and Nano projects exemplified this philosophy. These weren't just product launches; they were statements about trusting young teams to pursue multi-billion dollar goals.

Importantly, this wasn't a perfect science. Mukund acknowledged that Tata "made a number of mistakes. Some famous ones that really boomeranged badly on the group." Yet these setbacks were viewed not as failures of the philosophy but as necessary costs of developing future leaders.

Furthermore, Mukund writes, "During my years with him, Ratan Tata would consistently display a tendency to identify extremely talented individuals from outside the Tata group, often with some inbuilt angularities, personality quirks or sharp elbows, and thrust them on professional managers in the companies."

The impact of this approach went beyond individual careers. It created what Mukund called "so much opportunity and such a transformation that can make in your life if you get responsibility and a challenge given to you when you have the energy, the passion, and youth on your side."

This philosophy extended into Tata's later years, when he engaged with startups. He was drawn to "the kind and quality of work that young people are doing, the risks they are willing to take."

As organizations globally grapple with attracting and retaining young talent, the Tata way offers a compelling alternative blueprint: trust them with real responsibility, back their big ideas, and accept that true empowerment comes with both risks and rewards. As Mukund reflected, this philosophy accelerated not just careers but character: "I think it helped me to grow as an individual much faster and to mature early on in my career."

The making of a global leader

As India aspires to take its place on the global stage, the Tata playbook offers invaluable lessons. When Mukund was asked about advice for Indian companies going global, his response was characteristically direct: "Global markets are brutal... you have to be aware that you have to make the full commitment. You have to be all in."

This "all-in" approach means investing in technology,

understanding local regulations (which can "catch you off guard"), and building market capabilities. Perhaps most importantly, as the Tata experience shows, it means having the patience to play the long game while staying true to your core values.

As Mukund reflected on his 23-year journey with the group, one thing became clear: the Tata way isn't just about what you do but how you do it. Whether it's waiting for the right time to list TCS, standing firm on ethical principles in aviation deals, or giving young talent real responsibility, the focus has always been on building something that lasts.

In an era where quarterly earnings often drive decisions and startup valuations dominate headlines, the Tata way offers a different paradigm: one in which patient capital, ethical leadership, and social purpose aren't just nice-to-haves but fundamental building blocks of lasting success.

For the next generation of Indian companies looking to make their mark globally, the message is clear: winning beyond boundaries isn't just about market share or valuations - it's about creating institutions that stand the test of time while staying true to their values.

Chapter 9
From Mathematics to Masa

Alok Sama's Guide to Global Success

In the summer of 2016, as global markets wrestled with Brexit uncertainty, Alok Sama orchestrated what would become one of technology's most audacious bets: SoftBank's $32 billion acquisition of ARM Holdings, driven by Masayoshi Son, the enigmatic visionary founder of SoftBank. The deal embodied everything that defined his tenure as SoftBank's CFO and President: bold vision, precise execution, and an uncanny ability to see value where others saw risk.

Yet when asked about the most memorable advice he received from Masa-san, as he is popularly known, during those high-stakes years, Alok responds with characteristic wit, "After you're 50, every time you pass the restroom, just use it."

This disarming humor is quintessential Alok, a man who navigated life's most "bizarre" moments—his word, not ours—with a mix of sharp intellect and wry humor.

Whether orchestrating multi-billion-dollar mergers, weathering elaborate smear campaigns, riding the tech bubble's dizzying highs, or enduring its crushing lows, Alok has approached each challenge with a blend of measured wisdom and levity.

His extraordinary journey is chronicled in his riveting best-seller, The Money Trap: Lost Illusions Inside the Tech Bubble, a book that reads less like a corporate memoir and more like a thrilling account of the wild west of global tech investing, with some truly heart-touching personal anecdotes.

Before masterminding monumental deals like the Sprint and T-Mobile merger or the landmark acquisition of ARM, Alok spent his childhood in Delhi's AIIMS quarters, sporting a thick black bouffant inspired by Amitabh Bachchan. (That hairstyle reportedly cost him admission to St. Stephen's College's economics program, but that's a story for another day. Or better yet, read his book!)

What began as a burning desire to solve Fermat's Last Theorem evolved into a career tackling complex challenges that would shape the modern tech landscape.

Yet, beyond the billions and boardrooms, Alok Sama's story offers a masterclass in navigating global markets while maintaining authentic leadership. Here are five key lessons from his remarkable journey, both personal insights and wisdom gained alongside Masa-san, that reveal what it takes to succeed in today's complex global landscape.

Lesson 1 - Embrace serendipity, but stay prepared

"You cannot connect the dots looking forward; you can only connect them looking backwards," said Steve Jobs in his famous 2005 Stanford Commencement Address.

Alok Sama would agree.

The first "dot" appeared when his father requested his friend to speak with Alok.

Picture a young mathematics graduate in Delhi, consumed by an obsession to solve Fermat's Last Theorem, unaware that a single conversation would soon alter the course of his life.

His father's friend turned out to be Dr. Shiv Gupta, a statistics professor at Wharton, an institution Alok had never heard of. For the young maths enthusiast, Gupta's description of an American MBA and potential earnings of $40,000-50,000 a year seemed like a fantasy. Yet this conversation would become the first in a series of strategic inflection points.

The second dot emerged through his friend Sanjeev Bhikchandani (yes, the OG founder and executive vice chairman of Info Edge). Sanjeev had already taken the GMAT and saw the same potential in Alok that Dr. Gupta had identified. "You should do this too. Maybe your father can afford to pull this together for you," he said - words that would prove prophetic.

What followed was a series of connections that would prove transformative. At Morgan Stanley, it was an Indian immigrant managing director who saw potential in Alok and helped launch his investment banking career.

> ***"Networks are really important," Alok reflected, tracing how these cultural connections facilitated each pivotal moment in his career.***

The most pivotal connection emerged through Nikesh Arora, now CEO of Palo Alto Networks and then heir apparent to Masayoshi Son. While their shared Delhi background - Nikesh's father in the Air Force and Alok's at AIIMS - created initial rapport, their intellectual wavelength turned a cultural bond into a powerful professional partnership. In global business, where cultural fluency can be as crucial as financial acumen, such relationships often mark the difference between good deals and great ones.

"With Nikesh, it was also a case of his analytical ability to process… I've never seen anything like it," Alok recalled. "If you're in a room with him and keeping pace with him, you can give yourself a pat on the back."

Their dynamic was so strong that occasionally, Alok would even be a step ahead–a feat both men came to appreciate. This combination of cultural connection and intellectual rapport eventually led to Alok's role at SoftBank, where he orchestrated some of tech's largest deals.

For aspiring global dealmakers, Alok's journey illuminates a crucial truth: while serendipity creates opportunities, it's the combination of intellectual rigor, cultural intelligence, and strategic relationship-building that transforms chance encounters into billion-dollar deals.

Lesson 2 - Master the time machine strategy

In the world of tech investing, everyone's looking for the next breakthrough innovation. But as Alok Sama revealed, Masa-san's genius lies in a deceptively simple approach: the time machine strategy.

"It's very straightforward," Alok explained, debunking the mystique around SoftBank's investment philosophy.

> *"No magic in this. It's not like Einstein and time travel or whatever. It's simple. Look*

> ***at disruptive models that have worked elsewhere, whether it's transportation or fintech, and transport them to emerging markets like India. With modest tweaks, it should work."***

The strategy's elegance lies in its risk-reward profile: proven business models, untapped markets, and precise timing.

What makes this strategy especially relevant is India's unique position in the global economy. As Alok explained, "India is a giant market. You are operating in one of the most cost-sensitive markets in the world. So, if you've found a way to make money here, you should be able to transport that elsewhere."

He illustrated this point with the example of Sunil Mittal's Bharti Airtel: "Operating in India, where your ARPUs are a fraction of ARPUs in China, lower than in Africa. Think about that. It's mind-blowing. And they've been profitable and phenomenally successful."

The beauty of the Time Machine strategy lies in its pragmatism: rather than betting on unproven innovations, it focuses on proven models implemented by battle-tested entrepreneurs when a market is ready to scale.

The success of this strategy is evident in companies like Ola. As Alok explained, "You don't have that much of a public transportation infrastructure in most Indian cities, so the need for an Uber-like alternative is natural." This creates what he called, "a secular trend that's there to stay for the next 10, 20, 30 years."

Lesson 3 - Embrace your crazy

When asked about what makes Masa-san unique, Alok Sama pointed to what he calls "the crazy factor" – a unique quality that sets truly visionary entrepreneurs apart.

While the "crazy" might vary, all truly world-class entrepreneurs have it and embrace it wholeheartedly.

These entrepreneurs possess a superpower-like ability to see the future before others do.

> *"You look at the greats out there, and I put Elon Musk in there, they have that quality. That's really, really rare," Alok emphasized.*

The roots of this visionary quality in Masa-san's case run deep, shaped by early adversity. "Being a Korean in Japan is like being the absolute bottom end of the caste system in India," Alok explained. "It literally was that ugly. And I have to believe that made an impact."

Son's track record of predictions is nothing short of remarkable. "When people talk about Masa-san being a one hit wonder with Alibaba, I say it's bullshit," Alok stated emphatically.

He listed Son's big bets: "You talk about the PC revolution. (He was the) distributor of Microsoft software in Japan. He called that. The internet, he called that. He became the richest man in the world. Mobile phones and smartphones taking over the world… he called that. He was talking about AI 10 years ago."

Even Son's missed bets reveal the depth of his visionary thinking. The Nvidia saga stands as a testament to this. "I ran the numbers and even made judgments as to if you had to buy

Nvidia, it would have cost us $83 billion," Alok recalled. "And talking to Masa and saying, 'Son San, absolutely, let's go for it! This makes so much sense,' Because this was Masa at his best, right? Calling a technology trend and saying, 'okay, the stock's expensive, but the market doesn't get how big this is going to become."

The obstacle, however, was that "there was no way CFIUS (Committee on Foreign Investment in the United States that reviews foreign investments in the US companies to assess potential national security risks) would not allow a foreigner, even though it is a friendly Japanese, to take control of an asset like Nvidia. So, we bought a public stake of less than 5%."

This ability to see beyond current valuations to future potential defines truly visionary leaders. As Alok noted, drawing a parallel to another tech visionary, "Look at some of the deals that Mark Zuckerberg did even when they seemed outrageous. WhatsApp is the ultimate example..$19 billion. It turned out to be a phenomenal deal. Insta(gram) is even better. Brilliant in terms of predicting and hedging its future in terms of where social networks were headed, which is visual and mobile. You have to make judgments about how habits will evolve. But equally, it is that self-belief (too). I can justify it because what I'm after is worth a trillion." That's the essence of the 'crazy factor' – the courage to act on conviction when conventional wisdom says you're wrong.

Lesson 4 - Learn the art of global deal-making

When asked about his most challenging deal, Alok Sama didn't hesitate, "It's Sprint and T-Mobile because I was in a quasi-principal role. I wasn't just advising someone. There's a lot at stake. It was almost existential in terms of that Albatross hanging over Masa's neck."

The multi-billion merger offers a fundamental lesson about deal-making:

> *"Deals are all about figuring out what's crucially important to you, where you are willing to compromise, and what the other side is willing to compromise on."*

This isn't just textbook wisdom but a hard-earned insight from orchestrating one of tech's largest deals. "You can never approach a complete win-win, but you can at least get to a point where both sides get a piece of what's really, really important, and what they've compromised on is what's less important to them," he explained.

Alok draws a crucial distinction between the two types of M&A deals. The first type, exemplified by Sprint/T-Mobile, is driven by strategic necessity. Alok said it was the "case of two companies that needed to get together to create a viable competitor. It was literally as simple as that." The deal's success came from identifying clear synergies.

"Sprint had a ton of spectrum. T-Mobile had an amazing marketing-oriented management team. They built a brand that is terrific and very popular among millennials."

Then there are the visionary bets, like SoftBank's acquisition of UK-based chip designer Arm Holdings in 2016. "That's a uniquely Masa Son deal. No synergies whatsoever. That deal was a giant bet on technology and a vision of the future."

These deals are particularly challenging because "you pay this hefty premium. The market doesn't get it, or the market doesn't believe it."

So we paid this hefty premium above market value and the market value of SoftBank declined by the exact amount of that premium.

These two approaches to deal-making – strategic necessity versus visionary bets – represent the full spectrum of what's possible at the highest levels of global M&A. Together, they reveal that true deal-making mastery lies not just in knowing how to negotiate but in understanding which type of deal you're in and what that demands of you.

Lesson 5 - Be intellectually curious

At 58, most successful global executives are planning their retirement. Alok Sama was planning his next classroom adventure.

"I got a master's degree in Creative writing from NYU at age 58," he shared, describing what he calls "a brave thing to do, being in a classroom with a bunch of 28-year-olds." This wasn't just a retirement hobby – it was a manifestation of what Alok considers the most crucial quality in successful people: intellectual curiosity.

"The number one quality I look for when I interview people," he emphasized, "is intellectual curiosity. You almost take for granted smartness, etc."

This philosophy has shaped not only his career choices but also his approach to understanding the world.

His favorite writer, Vladimir Nabokov, said, "One cannot read a book; one can only reread it" – a principle Alok applies to both literature and business. "Whatever you are, whatever you see, try and figure out what's behind this. What's the story behind this?"

This perpetual learning mindset has served him well in a career spanning multiple technological revolutions and market cycles. From understanding complex derivatives well enough to explain them to former vice president of the United States, Dick Cheney, to grasping the implications of AI well enough to advocate for an $83 billion NVIDIA acquisition attempt by SoftBank, Alok's career demonstrates how intellectual curiosity transforms into business acumen.

For those aspiring to navigate the increasingly complex world of global technology and finance, the lesson is clear: technical skills may get you in the door, but it's intellectual curiosity that keeps you in the room where decisions are made.

Navigating a global journey

From solving mathematical theorems in the government quarters of AIIMS Delhi to orchestrating billion-dollar deals in SoftBank's Tokyo boardrooms, Alok Sama's journey offers more than just inspiration – it provides a blueprint for navigating the increasingly complex intersection of global finance, technology, and cross-cultural leadership.

Perhaps most tellingly, Alok points to a cultural trait that has shaped his approach: "This obsession with *gyaan*, knowledge, in every form in India. Just a very sincere desire for self-improvement… for social mobility. It's extraordinary. I don't see that anywhere." In an era where technology and globalization are rapidly reshaping traditional business boundaries, this emphasis on continuous learning and adaptation has proven increasingly valuable.

The future of global business will belong to those who combine deep domain expertise with cross-cultural fluency, as Alok has done throughout his career. In that light, his journey isn't just a success story—it's a preview of what tomorrow's tech leaders must embody.

Section 3
Sportspersons

Chapter 10
Igniting a Billion Dreams

The Neeraj Chopra Way

90 beats per minute.

It was the collective heartbeat of 1.4 billion people, measured by the wearable brand Noise, as Neeraj Chopra took his mark at the Paris Olympics. Javelin in hand, he stood ready to make history—again.

The word to note is *again*.

In a country where Olympic medals are as rare as summer snow and cricket dominates every playground conversation, Neeraj Chopra has done the unthinkable. He's won not one but two Olympic medals—a feat unprecedented in Indian athletics—with the promise of more to come.

Armed with nothing but a spear and iron resolve, this 27-year-old from Haryana has captured India's imagination in ways previously reserved for cricket's greatest moments. His story began not with dreams of Olympic glory, but with playground taunts. In the small village of Khandra, Panipat, a chubby teenager—nicknamed 'Sarpanch' (village elder) by his peers—walked into Panchkula stadium hoping merely to shed some weight.

What happened next defied every expectation. Among the

wrestling mats and boxing rings that typically attract Haryana's youth, young Neeraj's gaze fixed upon a single javelin. That moment of choice would reshape not just his destiny but India's sporting legacy.

In tracing Neeraj's path from that first day at Panchkula stadium to Olympic glory, his story reveals four crucial lessons. The first speaks to the power of embracing the unexpected.

Lesson 1 - Embrace unconventional beginnings

In Haryana, a state that breathes wrestling and bleeds boxing, choosing javelin throw wasn't just unconventional—it was almost unheard of. For young Neeraj, the journey began with a simple goal of losing weight. "Children of Haryana are fond of playing sports," he said, "but I did not know that I would become a professional athlete or reach the Olympics in any sport."

His youngest uncle first suggested visiting the Panchkula stadium after the gym where he had started to work out shut down.

> *"I don't know why I liked javelin. I just did. I felt I'd be prepared to do anything to succeed. I think it was destiny that made me do it."*

This unconventional choice demanded equally unconventional methods. Unlike European athletes with generations of javelin-throwing heritage to draw from, Neeraj and his early coaches had to figure things out as they went along.

Neeraj recalled that he trained in the 'desi way'—a mix of basic throws, jumps, and weight lifting for strength. "We didn't know that much here," he admitted, but this limitation forced creativity. Without established pathways to follow, they were free to experiment, adapt, and innovate.

The results were extraordinary. Within just two years, Neeraj shattered the national under-16 records, hurling the 700-gram javelin almost 70 meters. "It was my first national in javelin, and I made a national record in the first event itself," he remembered. That moment proved what would become a recurring theme in Neeraj's journey: sometimes, the path less traveled leads to unprecedented destinations.

Lesson 2 - A tree with strong roots can weather any storm

"You go ahead; we'll back you. We believe in your hard work."

In rural Haryana, where farming rhythms dictate daily life, Neeraj Chopra's family made an extraordinary choice. When their son picked up a javelin—they didn't just accept his decision; they embraced it wholeheartedly. His family's early vote of confidence became a cornerstone of his success as an athlete.

"It stays in the mind that the family trusts me. They trust my hard work," Neeraj reflected. "So, I put my maximum effort on the field."

Neeraj's extended family keeps him grounded, their support wrapped in the time-tested values of their farming heritage.

"I know how to do all the work," Neeraj said with pride. "Milking the cow, fodder cutting, I have done all 'A to Z' work. I still do when I'm home."

But his family's influence goes beyond his work ethic. Neeraj fondly recalled his childhood—from throwing his first school book into a well to accidentally setting fire to fodder storage. "They used to scold, they also explained, and they used to love, too. So, everything was balanced," he said. This blend of discipline and unconditional support created a foundation of confidence that would prove crucial in the years to come.

Even today, amidst international acclaim and Olympic medals, this family connection keeps him rooted. "Because I travel constantly, I do not get a chance to mix with everyone much. Whenever I come home, I live like I used to live earlier."

In a sport where success often demands uprooting oneself from family traditions, Neeraj's story shows how deep roots can actually fuel soaring achievements.

Lesson 3 - Maintain balance in both success and setbacks

"We have to 100% live the present moment," Neeraj Chopra emphasized, revealing a philosophy that has defined his career. "We have to focus on how much

hard work we can do right now and how much improvement we can make."

This balanced approach to both triumph and setback has become his signature.

This mindset was evident early in his career. When he set the national record in his very first Under-16 competition in Lucknow, throwing almost 70 meters, his response wasn't to dream of distant glory but to focus on the immediate path forward. "I was very happy and believed that, 'yes, I can do very well in the future. But I also knew that it would take time to reach there'."

By being balanced in the face of crisis and victory, he turned what could have been crushing disappointment into fuel for growth. In 2016, at just nineteen, Neeraj achieved something extraordinary—setting a world junior record with an 86.48m throw in Bydgoszcz, Poland. The distance wasn't just impressive; it matched the eventual bronze medal mark at that year's Rio Olympics. But there was a catch: he'd missed the Olympic qualification deadline.

"The disappointment was there," he admits. "But I felt that, 'Yes, I have now entered that league, and I have done something for my country.' That throw was quite good. If I had gone to the Olympics and had done that throw, then I could have won a medal." Instead of dwelling on the missed opportunity, he found perspective: "It was probably written in my destiny that the first Olympic medal that I'd win for the country would be Gold."

Perhaps most telling is his approach to close misses. In the September 2024 Diamond League in Brussels, Neeraj missed the Gold by 0.01 meters. Neeraj's throw of 87.86 m was agonizingly short of Grenada's Anderson Peters' 87.87 meters.

His response?

"Raat gayi, baat gayi" (It's a new day; let's look forward). What made this response even more remarkable was the hidden story: he had competed with a fractured hand.

"4-5 days before the (Brussels) event, I had a fracture in my hand during training," he revealed. "The doctor advised me to get it operated on as soon as possible as the bone had broken a little, and it was quite painful. The doctor advised me to not play and said that it is risky because many times I fall after the throw and my hand hits the ground. I said, 'No, I will control it'. I was trying my best to put in all my effort, but I was not able to put in enough because I was afraid of falling. Even then, it was a very good throw, 87m plus throw. But it fell short by one centimeter."

Perhaps nowhere was this balanced mindset more evident than in his Olympic performances. During his historic Tokyo 2020 Gold medal win, he refused to celebrate until the very last competitor had thrown. "If I assume the Gold is mine and someone scores more, it becomes difficult mentally because I'm already satisfied," he explained. This mental discipline proved invaluable when he later won Silver in Paris 2024. His response? A mature acknowledgment that while "only Gold can be better than Silver," every achievement deserves its moment of appreciation.

This approach—taking neither victory nor defeat too personally, finding lessons in both triumphs and setbacks—has become more than just a strategy. Neeraj has mastered the delicate balance of holding his dreams firmly while staying loose enough to adapt to life's twists.

Lesson 4 - Build the right partnerships

Every champion's journey is shaped by those who guide them. For Neeraj Chopra, this truth has played out through a remarkable series of partnerships, each adding a crucial layer to his evolution as an athlete.

The story begins in Khandra village with Jaiveer Singh, his first 'bhai-jaise' (brother-like) coach, who taught young Neeraj the basic grip of a javelin. At the Tau Devi Lal Sports Complex, coach Naseem Ahmad expanded his foundation, making him train with long-distance runners to build stamina and strength.

Late Gary Calvert, who guided Neeraj in 2016, saw something special in his technique. "The javelin throw is all about getting the longest movement of the throwing arm in the shortest amount of time," Calvert said. "Neeraj has an instinctive feel for the long movement."

Neeraj, too, remembered him fondly. "I got to learn a lot from him. He brought a lot of change at the beginning of my career."

However, his partnership with biomechanics expert Dr. Klaus Bartonietz would truly transform Neeraj's career. "With him, I have won medals in two Olympics, two World Championships, Diamond League, and Asian Games," Neeraj reflected. What made this partnership special wasn't just the technical expertise but the deep understanding they developed. Under Bartonietz's guidance, Neeraj found a coach who could adapt to his natural style rather than forcing dramatic changes.

This wasn't always the case. Earlier, working with the legendary Uwe Hohn—the only athlete to throw a javelin beyond 100 meters—presented both opportunities and challenges. While Hohn's strength-focused approach significantly improved Neeraj's power, it came at a cost. "The strength improved, but somewhere, we had to compromise with flexibility, and then the injuries started increasing," Neeraj recalled.

Neeraj's belief about coaching relationships is simple: technical expertise alone isn't enough.

> *"Along with training, you should also have an emotional connection," he explained. "I can work professionally, but there should be that bonding so that we can tell each other about our shortcomings."*

This philosophy extends beyond just coaches to his entire support system. His current physiotherapist, Ishaan Marwaha, travels with him constantly, ensuring his body stays in peak condition. It's about creating an environment where vulnerabilities can be shared, and trust goes beyond professional relationships.

Now, as he begins a new chapter with Czech javelin legend Jan Zelezny, Neeraj embraces both the excitement and challenges of change. "Sometimes we are in a comfort zone and think that everything is going well, but I feel that sometimes we should take a little risk," he reflected. This willingness to evolve while maintaining strong emotional connections has defined his approach to partnerships.

In the end, Neeraj's journey shows that the best coach-athlete relationships aren't just about technique and training—they're about finding mentors who can nurture both the athlete and the person within.

The golden boy

"Many people told me, 'No, you aren't capable of it,'" Neeraj recalled of his early days. Today, he has surely proven his nay-sayers wrong.

"With that belief, move in the right direction, work hard the right way... everything has to be done with good intentions," he emphasized.

When history looks back on his career, his most powerful achievement won't be measured in meters or medals—it will be in showing a billion Indians that when resilience meets destiny, even the most improbable dreams can take flight.

Chapter 11
Game. Set. Match.

The Man Who Redefined Indian Tennis, the Mahesh Bhupathi Story

6-4, 6-1.

The scoreboard at the iconic Roland Garros flashed these numbers as Mahesh Bhupathi and his Japanese partner, Rika Hiraki, had accomplished what seemed impossible just a few weeks before.

The unseeded pair, who had just about managed to enter their names minutes before the window closed, had just defeated the tournament's top-seeded American duo, Lisa Raymond and Patrick Galbraith, to win the 1997 French Open mixed doubles final.

This was the moment when 23-year-old Mahesh Bhupathi became India's first-ever Grand Slam champion—a title that had eluded a nation of one billion people for decades. More importantly, it was the beginning of a story about building an extraordinary career from scratch, armed with little more than raw talent and an obsessive drive to succeed. Incidentally the duo won the title on June 7, 1997, on Mahesh's birthday.

Over the next decade and a half, Mahesh would amass an incredible 12 Grand Slam titles, four in men's doubles and eight in mixed doubles. Along with India's other tennis legend, Leander Paes, he formed one of the most formidable doubles partnerships in tennis history, earning the nickname 'The Indian Express.' They, in fact, became the world's no.1 men's doubles team in 1999.

While an Olympic medal would remain frustratingly out of reach—a reminder that even the best-laid plans have their blind spots—Mahesh's impact transcended the boundaries of tennis courts.

Perhaps Leander Paes puts it best when asked to explain why this was so special.

"Maybe because until then, no Indian had become the No. 1 in the world in team sport. When Mahesh and I reached the top, we were pioneering through Indian sport to prove that there could be champions out of India. We were proving that we could be world-beaters. There was no know-how, no knowledge, no theory in the book to tell us how to do it. And that's what made it unique," said Leander in an interview with a leading Indian daily.

In a country where cricket is a religion and every other sport an afterthought, Mahesh Bhupathi showed that greatness knows no boundaries. He didn't just break barriers; he quite literally smashed them, creating a path where none existed and proving that Indian athletes could compete and win at the highest level of world sport.

But grand achievements rarely begin with grand moments. They often start in unlikely places: a father's dreams, a child's first grip on a racquet, and countless pre-dawn practice sessions. For Mahesh Bhupathi, this journey began even before he took his first breath.

Lesson 1- The power of obsession: When a family dreams as one

CG Krishna Bhupathi, Mahesh's father, was ranked as high as six in an era when Indian tennis boasted talents like Ramanathan Krishnan, Jaidip Mukerjea, Vijay Amritraj, and other stalwarts. Then came the car accident that shattered his playing career abruptly.

It was when Sr. Bhupathi made a decision that would seem almost maniacal to outsiders: his firstborn would be a tennis player, boy or girl. This wasn't a father's casual dream—it was a full-blown obsession that began in the waiting rooms of doctor visits. Mahesh's mother recalls being taken to tennis matches during her pregnancy so the unborn Mahesh could hear the sound of the ball hitting the racquet.

By age three, young Mahesh was wielding a badminton racquet as the tennis racquet was obviously too heavy for his tiny hands. The courts weren't his second home—they were his first. And somewhere between the countless hours of practice and his father's relentless passion, the obsession passed from one generation to the next.

When Mahesh was seven, the family moved to the Middle East, where he and his father were "literally the only two people with a racquet." What seemed like a devastating setback—no competition, no peers, no traditional path to success—became the foundation of an unconventional advantage.

While other parents chased junior rankings and quick wins, the father-son duo played a different game entirely. They focused on developing an aggressive style that would dominate the men's circuit, even if it meant Mahesh never cracked the top 10 in Indian juniors. It was a long-term bet on Mahesh's future.

A pivotal moment came when 12-year-old Mahesh visited Wimbledon. Standing in line for after-6 PM tickets, running into the hallowed grounds, and watching hours of tennis under the long British summer evening, young Mahesh had found his reckoning. "That's when it turned for me," he recalled. "I wanted to play there one day."

Little did he know then that he would not only play there but also lift the prestigious Wimbledon trophy with Leander Paes. That 1999 victory was part of an extraordinary season in which Lee-Hesh, as they were fondly called, reached the finals of all four Grand Slams, claiming both the French Open and Wimbledon titles. The 12-year-old's dream manifested into his destiny.

This tale of obsessive family support isn't unique to Mahesh. He points to another Indian tennis legend, Sania Mirza, whose father, a Ranji-level cricket player with no tennis background, made his daughter's tennis journey his family's mission when he saw her potential.

"Today, sport is so frightfully competitive and difficult to succeed in that it's impossible unless you're able to do that within your own ecosystem with obsessive support of your parents and family. It has to be a full-hearted process," Mahesh reflected.

Perhaps the greatest lesson from the Bhupathi playbook

isn't about tennis at all—it's about the raw power of collective conviction. When one person's obsession becomes a family's mission, impossible dreams don't just become possible; they become inevitable.

Lesson 2 - Seize moments that matter

Let's return to that pivotal moment at the '97 French Open. A 23-year-old Mahesh Bhupathi, ranked 55th in the world, was preparing to practice at Roland Garros. That's when his coach, Enrico Piperno, tossed out a casual suggestion—the kind that changes history before anyone realizes it.

"Why don't you sign in for mixed doubles?" Enrico suggested. "It's a couple of grand extra if you get in, plus accommodation per diem."

For Mahesh those extra grands seemed worth a shot. He scribbled his name on the sign-in sheet and headed to practice.

What happened next was pure serendipity.

With just five minutes left before the deadline, a diminutive Japanese player walked in. The ever-resourceful Enrico spotted Rika Hiraki—4'11" tall, ranked 26th in the world, and looking for a partner. He practically ambushed her, having to show her a photo of Mahesh because, back then, nobody knew his name. It was the definition of hustling. They became the last team to make the cut.

"We've made another two grand this week!" Enrico excitedly told Mahesh at practice.

Their first match was nearly their last. Down three match

points, they barely scraped through. Enrico didn't mince words: "You're the worst mixed doubles player I've ever seen in my life." It was the kind of brutal honesty that either breaks you or makes you dangerous.

But something magical was brewing. With each match, the unlikely pair got better. They found their rhythm, their understanding deepened, and suddenly, they were in a zone. Fourth seeds fell. Then, the second seeds. Finally, in the championship match, they defeated the top seeds.

The rookie pair who had entered for "a couple of grand extra" became Grand Slam champions. The player whose photo had to be shown because no one knew him had just become India's first-ever Grand Slam winner. All because someone saw an opportunity in a five-minute window.

> ***"In '97, every match was just a little better paycheck, and there was actually no pressure," Mahesh recalled. "It was just funny to watch all the top seeds trying to figure out who these people were, but we just enjoyed beating them."***

The magical fortnight in Paris remains a testament to a fundamental truth in sports and life: sometimes, the biggest opportunities come disguised as small chances. The key is to grab them when they appear, even if you've never done it before, even if you're the last one to make the cut, even if your coach thinks you're the worst he's ever seen.

After all, who could have guessed that chasing "an extra two grand" would be Mahesh's chance to earn a place in Tennis history?

Lesson 3 - Best partnerships are effortless

Jakarta, 1994. In a hotel lobby, an unexpected conversation was about to spark one of tennis's greatest partnerships.

Leander Paes, already one of India's biggest tennis stars, approached the (slightly) younger Mahesh Bhupathi with a proposition. His planned doubles partner, Japan's Shuzo Matsuoka, had pulled out. What Leander said next would set the tone for one of tennis' most formidable partnerships.

"The only reason I'm asking you to play is because I think we can win the tournament. Otherwise, I wouldn't waste my time."

Though Mahesh tried to play it cool, he was sold. What followed was pure alchemy. From that first Challenger tournament in Jakarta, they didn't just win—they dominated. Victory after victory, tournament after tournament, they built something that defied conventional wisdom.

The pair won three Grand Slam men's doubles titles, an astonishing 25 ATP Tour titles, and rose to world number 1. If that's not enough, they also hold the record for the longest streak of doubles victories at the Davis Cup (24 wins between 1997 and 2010).

Contrary to what one might think, what made their partnership special wasn't endless communication. It was something more innate, more intuitive. Mahesh explained, "Some teams need a lot of communication. Ours didn't." They understood their collective strength on the court. Even during rough patches when victories were hard to come by, they knew they would be unstoppable once they found their rhythm. It was tennis at its most elemental—two players moving as one, reading each other's minds, anticipating each other's moves.

This silent understanding became their superpower. It didn't matter whether they were top seeds or unseeded; their reputation preceded them. "Nobody wanted to play us," Mahesh said. "We were not a fun team to play against."

What's even more remarkable is that this chemistry didn't need constant nurturing. They could play separately on the tour for months, then reunite for a tournament and instantly click. It was like a switch waiting to be flipped. When Leander and Mahesh stepped on the court together, opponents knew they were in for a tough battle.

Lesson 4 - Playing to your strengths is more important than overcoming your weaknesses

At the 2004 Athens Olympics, Swiss maestro Roger Federer stood across the net—world number one, tennis royalty, and a man with something to prove. Just months after claiming the top ranking from Andy Roddick, Federer had arrived in Athens as the gold-medal favorite, only to suffer a shocking singles defeat to a young Tomas Berdych. Now, paired with Yves Allegro in doubles, he was hungry for redemption.

However, the strategy against Federer and Allegro was very clear: don't give the genius a chance to weave his magic.

> *"We took Roger out of the match," Mahesh recalled. "We did not hit one ball that we didn't have to hit to him. We attacked his*

opponent relentlessly where literally the guy wanted to cry."

This wasn't their first giant-killing act at the Olympics. They had already dismantled Andy Roddick and Mardy Fish, America's powerhouse duo, in a match that perfectly showcased Mahesh's class and belief in his game.

Take that crucial first-set tiebreak against Roddick and Fish. At 5-all, Mahesh had to serve against Roddick, one of the most fearsome returners in tennis history.

"If you put 85% second serve most of the time with Mahesh kicking a second serve and Leander at the net, you felt good about winning the point. But with Andy Roddick, I hit the second serve that hit the back of the line, right? Because I had to, otherwise, he's a world-class champion and he was going to make me suffer," remembered Mahesh.

It was a calculated risk, and it paid off.

This ruthless clarity about strengths and strategy became Mahesh's signature. After that first French Open victory, when his coach pointed out his tendency to target the male player, Mahesh turned this insight into an art form. He became "relentless" in exploiting opposition weaknesses, eventually becoming the only player in tennis history to win Grand Slams with seven different mixed doubles partners.

One might ask, how does one achieve such success with so many different partners?

The answer lay in Mahesh's crystal-clear understanding of his strengths. His backhand was his fortress, so he deliberately sought partners strong on the forehand side.

More importantly, he knew his role. "I would keep it stable. I was not going to do anything too fancy." While his partners–whether Leander, Todd Woodbridge, Mark Knowles, or mixed doubles partners like Sania Mirza, Mary Pierce, and Martina Hingis–were the shotmakers and playmakers, Mahesh provided the foundation. He made his serves, made his returns, and this combined stability and flair helped close out matches.

As Mahesh remarked,

"If you're not at it, building on your strengths and working on your weaknesses, there's no chance to get better. And I mean, it's just a mindset."

In a world obsessed with fixing weaknesses, Mahesh's career offers a different wisdom: true mastery comes not from being good at everything but from being unstoppable at what you do best. Sometimes, that's all you need.

Lesson 5 - Don't let your failures define you

Some defeats cut deeper than others.

For Mahesh Bhupathi and Leander Paes, the 2004 Athens Olympics remains that moment. "You don't recover from it," Mahesh admitted quietly.

The story has all the ingredients of a Greek tragedy.

After defeating tennis giants Andy Roddick and Roger Federer and dispatching the third-seeded Zimbabwean pair of Wayne Black and Kevin Ullyett, Lee-Hesh reached the semifinals. The remaining field consisted of pairs that were primarily singles specialists. Suddenly, the Indian Express had become the favorite for the gold medal.

The morning of the semifinal against Germany's Nicolas Kiefer and Rainer Schuttler started perfectly. The warm-up felt great. They expected to walk onto the court to Indian cheers. After all, the media was buzzing with anticipation of a potential gold medal.

Instead, they were greeted by a wall of sound from 4,000-5,000 German supporters. "It was the first jolt to the heart," Mahesh recalled. A perfect storm followed: pressure mounted, Kiefer's 'gamesmanship' got under Leander's skin, and their dream began unraveling in what Mahesh described as "a disastrous match."

The day between the semifinal loss and the bronze medal match was excruciating. Their families received special permission to visit the Olympic Village, but all that the duo wanted was solitude. When they stepped onto the court for the bronze medal match, they fought hard. The 16-14 final set score attests to that, but they knew something was broken. "Deep down inside," Mahesh reflected, "we fought hard, but it was still not going to be a win (even) if we (had) won that match."

Years later, Mahesh found himself explaining to young players why sports matter, even if you don't turn professional.

"The competition, how to deal with losses, how to react to winning, how to figure out when things are not going well and find solutions. It just teaches you a lot," he said.

Beyond the baseline: Building a legacy

Today, Mahesh's life has come full circle. Based in Dubai, he divides his time between building a sports and entertainment ecosystem with APL Apollo in Delhi and watching his daughter develop her own relationship with tennis. "I'm giving her all the tools," he says about her journey, echoing a philosophy that defined his career. "Everything else is up to her."

The cyclical nature of life isn't lost on him. Three decades ago, a father's obsession launched an unlikely tennis journey. Now, that journey's legacy rests in a more measured approach to the same sport. Between these two points lies a career that redefined what was possible in Indian sports—twelve Grand Slams, a world number-one ranking, legendary partnerships, and, yes, even defeats that taught more than victories.

But perhaps Mahesh Bhupathi's most enduring contribution isn't in the records he set or the titles he won. It's in proving that excellence doesn't always follow conventional paths. Sometimes, it comes from signing up for a mixed doubles tournament just for the extra money. Sometimes it comes from playing to your strengths rather than fixing your weaknesses. And sometimes, it comes from understanding that the greatest achievements aren't just about crossing boundaries—they're about smashing those boundaries that were always imaginary to begin with.

Sources

Chapter 2 : From Troll to Triumph: How Freshworks Conquered Global SaaS from India

https://blume.vc/podcasts/blume-podcast/s3-e01-building-a-3-5b-global-giant-from-chennai-to-nasdaq-girish-mathrubootham

https://archive.factordaily.com/longform/making-girish-mathrubootham/

https://www.freshworks.com/day-zero-for-freshworks-blog/

https://www.techinasia.com/freshdesk-founder-saas-superstar-girish-mathrubootham-ambitions-fears-secret-strategies

https://foundr.com/articles/leadership/how-girish-mathrubootham-turned-freshdesk-into-a-global-force

https://inc42.com/buzz/freshworks-revenue-jumps-19-to-153-mn-in-q3-sets-sight-on-1-bn-revenue-by-2026/

Chapter 3 : From Commodities to Consumer King: How Harsh Mariwala Transformed Marico into a Global Juggernaut

Harsh Mariwala and Ram Charan. Harsh Realities: The Making of Marico. New Delhi: Penguin Random House India, 2021.

https://blume.vc/podcasts/blume-podcast/s3-e03-scaling-marico-to-rs-86-000-crore-global-brand-harsh-mariwalas-winning-formula

https://economictimes.indiatimes.com/harsh-mariwala-steps-down-as-marico-managing-director/articleshow/32619267.cms?from=mdr

https://marico.com/india/about-us/overview

Chapter 4 : Nice Guys Win Big: Anand Deshpande's Contrarian Playbook to Build Generational Companies

https://www.forbes.com/profile/anand-deshpande/

https://www.persistent.com/media/press-releases/q4-fy24-results/

https://www.youtube.com/watch?v=uSIHi7APakA

https://blume.vc/podcasts/blume-podcast/s3-e05-how-anand-deshpande-built-a-9-billion-powerhouse-the-persistent-systems-story

Chapter 5 : From India to the World: The Hardware Revolution Led by GreyOrange and Ultrahuman

https://blume.vc/podcasts/blume-podcast/s3-e07-revolutionizing-make-in-india-ft-akash-gupta-of-greyorange-mohit-kumar-of-ultrahuman

Chapter 6 : Soaring High: Aditya Ghosh's Guide to Building People-Centric Companies

https://blume.vc/podcasts/blume-podcast/s3-e06-from-indigo-to-akasa-aditya-ghosh-on-winning-in-indian-aviation

Chapter 7 : The OG Bureaucrat Entrepreneur: How Amitabh Kant Engineered India's Transformation

https://www.nationalgeographic.com/traveler/articles/1028kerala.html

https://blume.vc/podcasts/blume-podcast/s3-e04-amitabh-kants-vision-for-indias-transformation-from-incredible-india-to-invincible-india

Chapter 8 : Built to Endure: The Tata Manual for Timeless Institution Building

The Brand Custodian: My Years with the Tatas

https://blume.vc/podcasts/blume-podcast/s3-09-tatas-400-billion-secret-ethics-innovation-leadership-ft-mukund-rajan-tatas-first-brand-custodian

Chapter 9 : From Mathematics to Masa: Alok Sama's Guide to Global Success

https://blume.vc/podcasts/blume-podcast/s3-e08-masa-mergers-and-making-it-big-ft-alok-sama-softbanks-deal-whisperer

The Money Trap: Lost Illusions Inside the Tech Bubble, Pan Macmillan

Chapter 10 : Igniting a Billion Dreams : The Neeraj Chopra Way

https://blume.vc/podcasts/blume-podcast/s3-e10-neeraj-chopra-from-haryanas-hinterlands-to-olympic-gold-inspiring-a-billion-hearts

https://www.news18.com/viral/this-data-shows-how-neeraj-chopras-javelin-throws-at-olympics-2024-drove-heart-rate-of-fans-9011320.html

https://olympics.com/en/news/india-javelin-throw-neeraj-chopra-coach-uwe-hohn

Chapter 11: Game. Set. Match. : The Man Who Redefined Indian Tennis, the Mahesh Bhupathi Story

https://www.hindustantimes.com/sports/tennis/our-friendship-was-at-its-lowest-when-we-were-standing-on-podiums-101631889541732.html?utm_source=chatgpt.com

https://scroll.in/field/1052012/watch-on-this-day-leander-paes-and-mahesh-bhupathi-won-the-wimbledon-doubles-title-24-years-ago

Scan the QR code to listen to the Blume Podcast S3.

Turn over to see how listeners reacted to this season's episodes.

WALL OF LOVE

"Love this! Must listen for founders building for the world."

A **Apurva Chamaria**
Global Head of Venture Capital & Startup Partnerships at Google

"An episode everyone should watch."

S **Siddharth Sharma**
Founder, YellowKyte
Co-Founder s11s.
Podcast Host
ReasonablyIrrational

"Very informative and inspiring👍"

S **Sivaram A S**
Vice President of Sales - Cavintek

"Lovely to see this!
Thanks for bringing the best founders on the pod 🚀"

J **Jivraj Singh Sachar**
Founder & General Partner (GP)
Indian Silicon Valley Capital

"Awesome Karthik. Way to go"

J **Jitendra Nayyar**
Chief Financial Officer, Oister Global + Euler Motor + Zupee

"Excited to watch this"

A **@ashish3354**
YouTube User

"That was a great interview with such a humble person. I'm glad I stumbled upon it unknowingly!"

L **@lazzybirdflying3225**
YouTube User

"GIRISH M anna always Great"

R **@rajeshvenk-atesan1999**
YouTube User

"Such a great conversation.
The candour and perspective was so refreshing. G didn't follow the playbook. He created it."

S **@shreevz**
YouTube User

A very informative episode into the mind of a successfull SAAS vanguard"

A **Abdur Rahman M.**
Software Consultant Freelancedev.in · Self-employed

"Fantastic conversation!"

C **@charanraj-an27**
YouTube User

"Great podcast, thanks a ton for doing this."

N **@nitinataustin**
YouTube User

"Loved it! Thank You Blume."

A **@adityaarsharmapersonal**
YouTube User

"Girish is becoming my Super Star!
Great insights and inspiring!"

D **@danielnirmalraj**
YouTube User

"Just listened to the whole thing. Loved every moment of it. So refreshing to see someone so accomplished talk plainly and not giving the "it depends" answer that most gyaandus give. You got a very special setting to do the interview too. Top-notch work as always, Karthik! 💎"

A **Blume Portfolio SaaS Founder**

"It's now all about skills , mindset , culture and vibes ...Blume Ventures"

N **Nivruti Gala**
Personal Branding Strategist
aka LinkedIn Ghostwriter

"Hey Karthik wanna share a small note but this may sound over ! But you're the hero of our Era! Building the home grown VC brand is just awesome ! I've been following Blume every intellectual channel ever since I was 18, three years ago, You Guys just Amazing! I've been learning news things daily ! Thanks For Challenging my curiosity I wish to work for Blume after completing my bschool journey from IIM."

V **@VigneshD-qv2os**
YouTube User

"Lovely how Girish bisects the layer of each question and tries to give detailed insights to the audience. He's not doing this interview just as an interview!"

V **@vijay-y5q**
YouTube User

"I watched this twice yes twice. I passed, processed, and went back 15 to 20 seconds a lot of times. Because this episode was that valuable, inside full and power pack. Kudos to Kartik for bringing the best out of Girish while keeping the core topic intact."

T **Tharun M**
SaaS Founder

"Girish Mathrubootham's journey with @FreshWorkInc is a masterclass in building a global product company from India. A must listen for aspiring product managers. There is so much to learn. #ProductManagement #Start-up Journey #BKartRed"

R **RKPadhy**
Professor, IIM Sambalpur

"Very insightful conversation!"

A **@AbCd-o2m8l**
YouTube User

"Brilliant Episode. Lots of nuggets of wisdom in it. Will do a rewatch some time this week."

S **Shravan TG**
SaaS Operator

"Amazing interview Karthik and Girish.."

R **@rprasannahsr**
YouTube User

"Thanks, Blume Ventures, for bringing this episode from a master storyteller!"

S **Shekhar Kirani**
Partner, Accel in India

"Dear Mr. Girish, you're an inspiration, Would love to meet you someday!"

K **@kcvinodkumar5122**
YouTube User

"Karthik, Loved the podcast that you hosted with G. The intro was super awesome. Love the prep work that you do...really comes across well 🙏"

A **Avinash Raghava**
Founder SaaSBoomi

"Time well spent on podcast with Girish, keep'em coming"

P **Portfolio founder**

"Man is a legend and so humble!"

A **@addy01999-ago**
YouTube User

WALL OF LOVE

"Bhupathi's story is a masterclass for founders/operators on building lasting partnerships, leveraging complementary skills, and bouncing back from setbacks. Highly recommend this podcast to all my students!"

R **RKPadhy**
Professor, IIM

"Great to see this kind of conversation. Keep bringing more from sports background"

S **@sayanbiswas_sports**
YT User

"Great advice"

Y **Yogesh Thakur**
Founder of "E Athlia" Sports App

"Amazing, glad to have made this association possible 🙂"

V **Vinay Singhal**
Co-Founder & CEO | STAGE

"Great episode, cheers to the whole team of Blume x STAGE :) "

P **Parveen Singhal**
Co-founder & CCO at STAGE

"Good one, folks. Wonderful associations. Congrats all around."

K **Kayar Raghavan**
Self employed, Director & Lead Investor

"Love his authenticity, so raw and no show off. Blume Venturese crushing with the content"

N **Nivruti Gala**
Personal Branding Strategist

"Totally refreshing Karthik B. Reddy"

N **Upasana Sharma**
Entrepreneurship Enabler & Learner

"His authentic simplicity is infectious."

G **Ganesh Sharma**
@erganeshsharma
1x.engineer | FOSS | DevOps

"Best athlete, inspiration of all young athletes"

D **@DiyaPareek-t1k**
YouTube User

"Best podcast I've watched in a while!"

M **@muskanbehune-g9z**
YouTube User

"Looking forward to this 🚀"

J **Jagadeash S**
Growth & Marketing Consultant @ Accel Atoms

"Best athlete, inspiration of all young athletes"

D **@DiyaPareek-t1k**
YouTube User

WALL OF LOVE

"Let's Go! Great Podcast from Blume! Keep Going 🔥"

S **@Soorya-ry6ov**
YouTube user

"Harsh's thought process around growth to motivate the team, shareholders, and every other stakeholder was very interesting. Very beautifully articulated. Thanks for bringing this out, Karthik."

B **Blume Portfolio Founder**

"This was a condensed masterclass on entrepreneurship. Easily among the best podcasts I have heard in a long time."

S **@sidharthnegandhi**
YouTube user

"Just listened to an inspiring podcast for aspiring entrepreneurs and managers! It demystifies myths around a truly Indian company with global vision. The message is clear: hire and nurture the best talent. Thoughtful questions, and heartfelt answers from a visionary."

R **RK Padhy**
Professor, IIM Sambalpur

"So much learning and inspiration.. Class podcast."

S **@74sgphotos39**
YouTube user

"Insightful"

V **Vaidyanathan K**
Senior Associate Director Central Procurement

"This is to congratulate you for the amazing podcast series that you host - I consume more podcasts than is healthy, and I think your podcast is the best business podcast in India. The Girish and the Mr. Mariwala ones were amazing. Thanks for doing that, and also the content your team puts out (the Indian enterprise SaaS playbook was super)."

A **Ashok Karanth**
Founder

"His emphasis on culture, lifelong learning, and giving back through the Ascent Foundation shows that his success is built on a foundation of continuous growth and community impact."

P **Parth Agarwal**
CEO at Maya Biotech India

"Real low profile LEGEND Harsh Mariwala is.. 🙏 Among the 3 giants Marico Limited is the only home grown 100% Bharat FMCG without any American or European ancestry"

V **V.G.Vignesh (VGV)**
Managing Director @ SaMaa Managing Partner @ IPA Associates

"Harsh has taken Marico to unprecedented heights, Shubbam.This is what inspired leadership does!"

S **Sanjeev Pendharkar**
Managing Director at Vicco Laboratories

"Insightful"

A **Akshay Dake**
CEO of VR ALUCAST

"Amazing leadership Harsh Mariwala!

H **Harveer Sahni**
Chairman at Weldon Celloplast Limited & author blog

"Wow, these nuggets of wisdom from Harsh Mariwala are pure gold! I especially love the idea of hiring people smarter than you. I tried that once, but they all kept correcting me, so I had to let them go. Kidding! But seriously, it's great to see a successful leader who values empowering their team."

M **monoo gupta**
Business Consultant

"It's extremely gratifying to know Indian born MNC is giving tough fight to established MNC's. More, importantly, leading brands and digital transformation."

Avadhanam Ramesh
Marketing Educator

"Love the way Marico embraced D2C! Seeing challenges as opportunities is a key mindset for staying competitive in today's ever-changing landscape."

Ashish Gupta
Marketing Director at Kanta Enterprises Pvt Ltd

"The most down to Earth person I've ever seen and his words are pearls of wisdom."

Tanveer S.
COO & MD - Premier Group- India

"Excellent. Marico has always given important to rural market from beginning."

Lalit Udeshi
Finance Controller at Franklin Wadcorpp India Pvt. Ltd

"These are such valuable insights, Shubbam Sharrma. Harsh Mariwala's commitment to lifelong learning and innovation is truly inspiring. His success is a testament to the power of continuous growth, experimentation and seizing new opportunities."

Akshay Jatia
Executive Director at Westlife Foodworld Limited

"Profound lessons"

Anish Bhatia
Founder and Chief Storyteller @Lemonz & @HappyFlash backs

"Useful tips"

Rajat Nayyar
VC Investment Advisor

"Insightful, looking forward to such posts. Request to include ROCE / ROIC as a parameter in the comparative analysis, for a holistic perspective. Best Wishes."

Satish Sundaram
Lead - HR / TA at Allyhealth Solutions

"Proud to be a mariconian once. Launching Honey was a thrill ride."

Vishal Singh
Sales @ Healthcare Medico

"Such an outstanding episode! Harsh Mariwala's ability to outsmart global competitors by focusing on overlooked opportunities in the FMCG sector is a masterclass in innovation. His leadership transition approach of 'hands-off, mind-on' is something every entrepreneur should take notes on.
Excited to hear more about how his unconventional talent strategies, and his views on the D2C revolution.
This is definitely going to be a weekend listen! Blume Ventures"

Nivruti Gala
Personal Branding Strategist aka LinkedIn Ghostwriter. Clients: Founders × VCs

"Karthik B. Reddy and Blume Ventures , thank you for the podcast. You won't believe it but while watching your podcast, I sit taking a pen and note book pausing every now and then to take notes! Big fan! Great learning! Thank you!"

Kundan Kumar Thakur
Assistant General Manager - Koncepo Scietech International

"This was a condensed masterclass on entrepreneurship. Easily among the best podcasts I have heard in a long time."

@sidharthne-gandhi
YouTube user

"What a lovely episode! I did not know what to expect, but I couldn't pause the video and finished it all in one sitting. The genuineness of both the host and guest shines through the episode."

@AdiPatil-nn8rk
YouTube user

"So much learning and inspiration.. Class podcast."

@74sgphotos39
YouTube user

"As a company dedicated to innovation and technological advancement, we at Brahma Labs find great inspiration in Harsh Mariwala's journey with Marico. His strategic approach to market domination, focus on differentiation, and commitment to continuous learning resonate deeply with our own values. Particularly noteworthy is Marico's adaptability in embracing D2C startups and digital transformation, areas where we specialize in providing cutting-edge solutions. It's refreshing to see how traditional businesses can evolve and thrive in the digital age, a transformation we're proud to facilitate for our clients. Thank you for sharing these valuable insights from a true pioneer in Indian business."

B **Brahma Labs**
LinkedIn user

"OMG such a wonderful discovery, harsh is really a star, pioneer among entrepreneurs. So much learning. Thanks"

R **@ravindersyal6613**
YouTube user

"Thank you to Mr. Mariwala for sharing these hard earned insights, thanks also to the Blume team for curating! So inspiring to learn from one of the best Indian entrepreneurs . 🙂🙏"

C **@ckcariapp**
YouTube user

"Perfect combination of ambition and humility...thank you for this podcast"

B **@bhaskarbhattacharya3566**
YouTube user

"Thank you for sharing such an amazing podcast episode. I truly enjoyed learning from Mr Mariwala's journey and found the insights incredibly valuable. Looking forward to more episodes like this!"

B **@yashaswinisharma440**

WALL OF LOVE

"Insightful"

A **Professor Arun Kumar Tyagi**
Emeritus Scientist, Uttarakhand State Council of Science & Technology, Dehradun, India

"Always insightfull to know more from you regarding India Visionary journey. Thanks Amitabh Kant sir for sharing this!"

R **Rohit Mishra**
Energy Utilities | NPCL| Ex Adani|Ex Big 4| Ex Torrent

"Insightful"

G **Dr.G.V. RAO**
Senior Advocate, Supreme Court of India & Ex-Vice-President, Indian Society of International Law

"Great episode Amitabh Kant sir! The conversational format really brings out the details and second order questions people have."

A **Aalekh Sharan**
Sarvam AI | BCG (Bay Area) | Eightfold | Aarogya Setu | CoS @ NITI AAYOG | IIT Delhi | Chicago Booth

"At 33 min, I loved the 3 qualities for leadership: (i) being an optimist, (ii) think big, say over a 15 years horizon, and (iii) the drive to change the system. Given the demographic dividend, we really need to be creative in providing quality education & skilling, at scale and low cost."

G **Gaurav Raina**
Professor, Electrical Engineering, IIT Madras

"Excellent vision."

G **gurucharan rani**
Financial Services Professional

"Amitabh Kant's vision for भारत economic growth is truly inspiring. The goal of achieving a $30 trillion economy by 2047 is ambitious but achievable with the right strategies in place."

V **Vipin Vaidya**
Assistant Manager at T3 & Itvar

"What an interesting approach towards development of tourism..really informative!!"

S **Samridhi Nema**
Research Associate | GoMP | Policy-Making | Legal professional

"Very informative"

A **Amar Kumar Swain**
Senior Manager Technology Consulting at EY

"We need multiple people like Amitabh Kant in our bharatavarsha."

K **@krishnakanthgriddaluru-8818**
YouTube user

"Truly said!"

V **Ved Kale**
e-Yantra's Robotics Challenge (23-24) - AIR 10 | Ex Intern @NIKOL EV, Pune | Learning & Exploring Core Electronics ⚡| Student Member - IEEE

"So good to hear him!! My all time fav. Amitabh Kant g"

B **Bhaawna A**
LinkedIn user

"Striving for a Viksit Bharat and a $30 trillion GDP goal by 2047 requires unparalleled entrepreneurship and innovation across sectors. Amitabh Kant's insights on India's economic journey are truly enlightening and offer valuable lessons for all of us."

M **Migi Chuang**
Company Owner | MBA in International Business

"Beautiful interview with Amitabh Kant! Loved it - Kudos - some lovely insights esp towards the end on how to build high performance teams awesome Karthik! "

A **Anand Sivaraman**

"Extraordinary"

B **Bimal Julka**
Arbitrator & Dispute Resolution Expert, Former Chief Information Commissioner (IAS Retd.)

"Really insightful!"

B **Binu Zachariah**
Social Entrepreneur

"What a great takeaway as a listener...carefully curated questions by the host and a truly inspiring honourable guest, Mr. Amitabh kant.."

A **@AnjanaSRaj**
YouTube user

"Insightful"

A **Aashish Benjwal**
AgileCoach, Gen AI Automation SME, Mentor Chapter Lead and E2E Automation Expert - Channels and Content

"Really Very Happy to Listen to this Pod Cast SPECIALLY MOTIVATION OF AMITABH KANT GOD BLESS WE WILL ACHIVE OUR GOALS"

A **@anantjajal5778**
YouTube user

"Thank you. I have subscribed."

N **@nnbg8000**
YouTube user

"This is a fascinating interview of an IAS officer . Clearly, Mr Kant is a doer (karma yogi) and we need more IAS officers like him. I wish him good health and long service for mother India 🇮🇳."

D **@dbiswas123**
YouTube user

"Very fascinating conversation.. Loved it thoroughly."

K **@kevnjanc**
YouTube user

"Amitabh Kant ji is a unique public centered Bureaucrat Leader with great & successful initiatives, as mentioned. Pray we that we have more such burreaucrats who make the difference to people's lives while taking Bharat ahead."

R **@ravikouljalali8831**
YouTube user

"Mr Kant will never be forgotten for the service to the Nation. Blessings 💕🇮🇳🙏"

K **@kutzchik**
YouTube user

"Great interview...Thanks"

R **@ravichandransivara-man6106**
YouTube user

"Amazing Interview 👍"

A **@ashhere31**
YouTube user

"What an insanely cool guy"

K **@kunalpareek8321**
YouTube user

"Great Man working with the great Government"

R **@rrs1902**
YouTube user

"he is a gem 💎"

S **@sasanka7474**
YouTube user

"Excellent video. I came to know about NITI UDYOG."

A **@AshokkumarTV-c8i**
YouTube user

"Excellent conversation"

E **@eather2023**
YouTube user

"Was a fantastic watch! Very interesting & motivating to know a person can take a negative situation (punishment posting) and turn it into a remarkably positive outcome! Really enjoyed the way you framed the questions"

F **Blume Fund IV Founder**

WALL OF LOVE

"Anand Deshpande beautifully captures the three qualities that define anyone in the arena - vision, resilience and embodied energy.."

P **Prachi Pandit**

"Always thankful to have deep insights."

N **Navdeep Singh Gill**
Global CEO XenonStack

"Deeply Understand your Ideal Customer."
Used to practice this principle in our business reviews, but now that you have coined a phrase for the same, it will help us build it as a DNA.
Thanks for the insights."

S **Sandeep Tapaswi**
CEO, Fands Infonet.

"This is very insightful and interestingly the orbit theory which highlights the Persistent journey through various phases (orbits). There is much to learn from this, whether one is looking to start a company or simply apply these lessons to life in general."

V **Vijay Madhav Pathak**
Architect Persistent Systems

"Very insightful episode 👍.."

R **Rahul Dhond**
CWM® Capital Markets | WealthTech

"Love your choice of guests..
Full of wonderful insights Blume Ventures"

N **Nivruti Gala**
Personal Branding Strategist

"I also recommend Anand's recent podcast episode with Blume Ventures - for plenty of nuggets from Persistant's journey and the second orbit program that he teaches."

R **Ramanand Janardan**

"Excited for this one."

N **Namma Bengaluru Startups**
LinkedIn user

"Amazing and informative notes!"

T **Tushar Borole**
Director - Architect UBS

"Great advice for aspiring technology leaders.
Thank you Anand Deshpande Sir"

A **Anand Agrawal**
CTO, Probus Insurance Broker Private Limited

"Beautiful sir. Thank you very much."

S **Sanjeev Sinha**
Principal Architect Persistent Systems

"I heard entire interview; It was a master class for early stage founders building companies; Anand Deshpande - thank you so much."

R **Raghu Babu Gunturu**
Founder at SimplyBiz

"always a pleasure listening to Anand Deshpande"

S **Samir Karande**
Founder and CEO at zOpt.ai

"Brilliant point of view, Anand Deshpande!
Thank you for sharing!"

M **Maneesh Joshi**
Founder and CEO, salesDNA.ai

"Inspiring Anand Deshpande Sir, How each of 150 CEO's appointment shaped up the understanding hashtag#howCEOsthink , as always delighted to see the insights and knowledge you share 👏"

N **Neerav Shiralkar**
Business Analyst Consultant at Estee Lauder Inc via Valtech

"Thanks for having a persistent Dr. Anand Deshpande roll out his journey in a humble way...nice questions in a humble way, good listening, giving time for the guest to make up his thoughts and deliver as a calm stream of events leading to a wonderful podcast. Great learning in all...Pranams to Blume"

R **@ravichandransivaraman6106**
YouTube user

"Great insights and wonderful questions that kept the conversation going without a boring moment!"

A **@AllenThomasVarghese**
YouTube user

"Persistent stock price has gone up almost 20 times in the last 4 years, since Covid i.e. Thanks Blume Ventures for such a wonderful discussion with Mr. Deshpande who has built a highly respected, and consistently profitable company."

K **@kedarrahalkar8741**
YouTube user

"Very informative Anand Deshpande"

A **Anil Godbole**
Helping Organization in Business transformation journey
AnZWORKS

"Great insights. Thanks for sharing."

S **Saurabh Pangarkar**
CEO & Founder @ Zime Solutions

"Super useful insight and advice!"

Y **Yogesh Kulkarni**
Co-founder & Director @ Altizon

"Great insights sir. Thanks for sharing!"

S **Srikrishna Arangode**
Tata Consultancy Services, Lead Project Manager (Automotive New Product Introduction)

"Highly Insightful sir.."

M **Meherzad Bhathena**
Project Manager, Persistent Systems

"This is great advice!"

N **Nikhil Karkare**
Product Owner
Effetrix Systems Pvt Ltd

"Very informative"

S **Shreya Maheshwari**
Infopercept Consulting, Sr. Client Engagement

"Valuable words."

L **Loukik Thakar**
ICICI BANK Private Banking, Private Banking & Family Office

"Insightful and very helpful"

P **Pavan Dikondkar**
Chief Cyber Security Consultant, Caze Labs Private Limited

"Very inspiring Anand Deshpande!"

S **Shreyas Karanjkar**
Co-Founder & AI Consultant @Axia

"Very informative!"

P **Parag Metha**
Software Development Manager SAS R&D India

"Amazing insights"

V **Vikram Sathaye**
Cricket Presenter, Standup Comedian

"Useful tips"

A **Anil Madule**
Senior Business Development Leader for the Americas at Pratham Technologies

"Thanks for sharing."

R **Rohit@pathintegral0**

"Very informative interview"

L **@Life_is_everything**
YouTube user

"Insightful"

V **Vaibhav Chipte**
Sr. Vice President Delivery, Onward Technologies Limited

"Great advice."

K **Kapila Maligaspe**
Regional Head Product services and Support Accelerite

"Respect!🎉"

B **@beautiful-musicforg-oodmood**
YouTube user

"Down to earth person"

R **@Ravikumar-cl1zu**
YouTube user

WALL OF LOVE

"An accidental encounter with pure knowledge... enjoying it... Thank you, Blume team, for curating these insightful podcasts with India's leading business personalities. Your dedication has created a treasure trove of knowledge for entrepreneurs and business owners. Keep up the fantastic work and continue to enlighten us. Thank you Karthik B Reddy for the learning."

S **Sravanan Viswanathan**
MIM, ARM

"Karthik, loved the episode with Mr Ghosh. One of your best."

N **<name missing>**
Pipeline Co-founder - Ex Baine - Bharat (SN knows)

"Very insghtful , amazing to see a C Suite with such high values."

A **@apramit**
TouTube user

"Podcast was mind-blowing."

C **@ImChekku**
Twitter user

"Brilliant interview. Congratulations to both of you 😊👍🙏"

S **@sharan50000**
YouTube user

"Insightful conversation!"

D **@devenparikh7004**
YouTube user

WALL OF LOVE

"So true!!!!! This is what evolutiond does to you -> Realization and acceptance."

S **Shiv Mamidi**
Manager, Enterprise Finance Reporting & Analytics, Intelligent Automation (RPA)

"Seems an amazing conversation"

N **Nivruti Gala**
Personal Branding Strategist ..aka LinkedIn Ghostwriter

"Incredible journey Akash Gupta ! More power to you and your team 💪"

V **Vikram Gupta**
Heading AI @ Minus Zero

"Very informative."

A **Ann Sun**
Key Account Manager/ Industrial Automation/ AMR/SMART WAREHOUSE

"I am enjoying the podcast Akash Gupta and Mohit Kumar. Blume Ventures thanks for hosting this. Very inspiring!"

D **Dipanjan Das**
LinkedIn user

"Akash Gupta: Smart and ethical, plus truly living his brand (grey = brains , orange = fun.) Congrats on all you and the GO team have accomplished!"

T **Terrie O'Hanlon**
Global Chief Marketing Officer, Agilysys

"This statement resonates so true:
"For premium products, customers aren't just buying hardware - they're buying a journey with the company" "

F **Frank Kotrus**
Director Business Transformation, IBM

"Such an inspiring story of global innovation and determination!"

S **Savings Dekho**
LinkedIn user

"These are amazing journeys from 2 of the exceptional founders."

A **@abhishek_ux**
YouTube user

"Thanks for the pod. Very insightful"

A **@adityak -5635**
YouTube user

"Good job. Hope more Indian's enter this field"

S **@srinidhira -o1620**
YouTube user

WALL OF LOVE

"In addition to mechanics & dynamics of mega deals, mindset & practices of stakeholders in the deals is the real insight from Alok Sama. Thanks for the first hand account."

S **Shyam Lal Singh**
Chairman & CEO, Planner India Assets Management , Venture Building & Investing

"Looking forward to listening. Alok Sama is a fascinating guy and a superb writer."

A **Andrew Bullen**
Retired

" Thank you Alok Sama.. Very insightful."

S **Sunil Haridas**
Founder and CEO @ Pradjna Intellisys, Founder & Vice President @ Kerala Startup Network (KSN-Global), Member @ CII Startup Panel, Kerala, Mentor @ Deep Tech Club, Nasscom and Atal Innovation Mission

"Great Podcast!"

S **@Soorya-ry6ov**
YouTube user

"Spot on Blume Ventures !!
Alok Sama beautifully highlights the delicate balance between control and acceptance. Key takeaways:
- Control is often an illusion, but luck alone isn't enough.
- Success lies in focusing on effort while letting go of what we can't control.
A refreshing perspective that challenges both extremes :)
Excited to listen to the full episode!"

N **Nivruti Gala**
Personal Branding Strategist ..aka LinkedIn Ghostwriter

"This is so true. Many thanks for sharing these wise words Alok."

A **Anurag Pathak**
Senior Vice President, HDFC

"I cannot get enough of Blume, you guys are really outputting real value"

S **@sufipasricha4106**
YouTube user

"This podcast was incredibly insightful!
My two main takeaways:
1. If a business model is disruptive in developed countries, with a few tweaks, it can thrive in emerging markets like India. A perfect example of this is Zepto—just a year ago, many were skeptical, but now it's clear that the quick commerce model is a game-changer, with every company pivoting in that direction.
2. If you can create and succeed in a cost-sensitive market like India, there's potential to scale and sell anywhere in the world.
Loved the discussion!"

S **@SahajRastogi**
YouTube user

"You guys are putting out bangers"

S **@SahilSanganis**
YouTube user

"Loved the Alok Sama podcast, great set of questions!"

A **Anirban Kundu**
Cred

WALL OF LOVE

"Podcast on Mukund's time in Tata
Today while travelling heard your subject podcast. Was a well-researched one and liked the way you went about it.

Keep up the good work. Never knew I could forget the jams on the Monday road.
I am surely going to tune in more frequently.

Happy Podcasting"

A **Wg Cdr (Dr) Ajay Kelkar (Veteran)**
Business Operations & Projects Head

"Very well reminisced & articulated 👏 Mukund Rajan 🌹👍 Mr. Ratan Tata 🙏"

P **Parmeswar Menon**
Co-Founder Director, CITENIK BIZNEZ LLP

"Very Insightful Mukund Rajan. Thank you for sharing."

S **Sheetal Arora**
Founder @ UpTroop - Whats App-first, AI-based Skilling Platform

"Good to see your recall, Mukund Rajan 😊"

S **@Sundar Raman S**
Client Success at Global PayEX

"Good to hear the achievements and Tata group's growth strategy."

K **Kannan R**
Corporate and Economic Advisor. Board Advisory (Global Services) . Indepedent Director. Member of Harvard Business Review Advisory Council.

"You're fortunate to have worked with a legend like Mr Tata."

N **Neeraj Kanoria**
Chairman at Indeevar Impex Pvt Ltd

"Mukund Rajan Always special to hear you Sir!!"

S **Smita Kudtarkar**
Co-Founder | Head Technology | Independent Director

"Listening you is just superbly fantastic Mukund!"

D **DK Gupta**
VP- Regulatory Legal, Vodafone Group India (C&W)

"A lifetime of memories Mukund. Thanks for enriching us with the share and insights."

S **Sarita Bahl**
Independent Board Director I ESG & CSR

"The point mentioned by Mr.Rajan about TATA's ethos as a company, that you work for a greater purpose, your hard work inturn benefits many more is truly remarkable."

P **@ponnushebin3802**
YouTube user

"Such a fascinating story"

N **Nivruti Gala**
Personal Branding Strategist

Acknowledgements

We want to take a moment to say thank you to everyone who made Blume Podcast Season 3 and this book possible.

- A big thank you to all Eleven guests for taking time out from their packed schedules for these conversations and to their teams/EAs for working behind the scenes to ensure the meetings happened;
- Special thanks to Vignesh J, Editorial Fellow at Blume Ventures, who authored the book from start to finish, often over the weekends and weeknights to meet the tight deadlines we set for ourselves;
- Deep appreciation for Shekhar Kirani, Partner at Accel, for his time and insights. A big thank you to Vatsal Srivastava, Head of Content and Communications at Accel, for making the conversation happen and for his input.
- A big thank you to Ann Mathew for bringing the best of her decades of design experience to create an elegant front and back cover.
- Special mention to Amit Mishra, Head of Global Sales and GTM-Software Businesses, Jio Platforms Limited,

for his valuable suggestion on the cover design.

- Brenelle Fernandes, EA to Karthik Reddy, for expertly finding the right slots for podcast recordings amidst Karthik's extensive travels;
- Ramanjit Kumar, our transcriber-in-chief, for providing us with accurate transcripts to consume and craft into this book;
- Mudit Narain of Blume Ventures for assisting in scheduling the interaction with Mr. Amitabh Kant;
- Vinay, Parveen, and the whole team at STAGE (Blume Fund III), for making the interaction with Neeraj Chopra happen. And also graciously letting us utilize their office for the shoot;
- The Admin staff at Blume's Mumbai office for helping us convert the lounge into a full-fledged podcast recording studio when needed;
- Last but not least, Aditya Kuber, Peter K, Aditya Mattoo, and the whole team at Ideabrews for producing the podcast series behind the scenes.

We hope you will join us in giving them a pat on the back and a virtual round of applause.

Core Team

- Karthik Reddy – Partner, Blume Ventures and Host, Blume Podcast
- Rohit Kaul – Marketing, Blume Ventures
- Vignesh J – Editorial Fellow, Blume Ventures
- Podcast Producers – IdeaBrews Studios
- Book Publishers and Distributors – Yashraj Sharma at Wyzr

About Blume Ventures

Blume Ventures is an early-stage India-focused venture fund that backs startups with both funding as well as active mentoring. Blume typically invests in Seed and pre-Series A rounds in tech-led startups led by founders obsessed with solving hard problems for the Indian market and from India for the world.

Blume presently invests out of Fund IV, a $290M vehicle supported by leading institutional LPs and family offices. With the close of Fund IV, Blume now has an AUM (Assets Under Management) of over $600m, managed by an investment team based across Bengaluru, Mumbai, Delhi, and San Francisco. Some of the leading startups we have backed included Purplle, Unacademy, Spinny, Ultrahuman, slice, Carbon Clean, and GreyOrange